D1429189

FAMOUS SCOTTISH HOUSES

HOLYROOD PALACE
FROM CALTON HILL

FAMOUS SCOTTISH HOUSES
The Lowlands

By

THOMAS HANNAN

M.A., F.S.A. (Scot.), Hon. C.F.
Author of "The Beautiful Isle of Mull."

WITH 101 ILLUSTRATIONS IN PHOTOGRAVURE

JAMES THIN

THE MERCAT PRESS
EDINBURGH

This is a reprint of the 1928 edition
ISBN 0901824 75 5

Printed in Scotland by
John G. Eccles Printers Ltd, Inverness

PREFACE

THE great houses of the land in which we live, whether in the English or the Scottish part of it, are intimately inter-woven with its history.

It is interesting to look upon some old ruined castle and to say—" Those desolate rooms and battlements were once the scene of strenuous life, sometimes warfare, sometimes gaiety, and they mark pages of history."

Many houses still inhabited are as old as some which are now ruins. There is a greater interest, to my mind, in an ancient house which is still a home than if it were a ruin; although, perhaps, the living house stimulates the imagination less than the ruin.

It may be a revelation to many to learn that in Scotland there is a very large number of houses which embody in their stones architectural features interesting or beautiful, sometimes both, which introduce to us great historical personages, and recall to us the supernatural legends of the past with the ballads and poetry of ages simpler than our own.

I have visited more than 150 houses of this kind in Scotland, and have left many more unvisited, in the course of numerous journeyings covering many years. This takes account only of houses which are still actual residences.

This volume treats of fifty such houses, either historic in them-selves or the successors of historic houses. They are not treated exhaustively in any one direction, but only enough in each case to give a fair idea of their interest. They are representative of the whole, but several volumes would not exhaust the list of equally representative and interesting houses which are still homes.

THOMAS HANNAN.

CONTENTS

vii

CONTENTS

ILLUSTRATIONS

All the illustrations, except the frontispiece and those facing
pages 14 and 15, are from photographs by the author.

FAMOUS SCOTTISH HOUSES

I

AUCHINLECK HOUSE, MAUCHLINE, AYRSHIRE

THIS old Scottish home is commonly known as Auchinleck House, but the ancient name was "The Place of Auchinleck," and the name sounds so much more interesting that I prefer to use it. The house and lands are in a very interesting part of Ayrshire, about eleven miles east of the town of Ayr and three miles south of the old town of Mauchline. In the history of the place there are four houses, and the remains of the three predecessors of the present residence are still to be seen—a remarkable chain, perhaps unique in Scotland.

The present house was designed by Robert Adam, whose birth centenary is in the present year ; and it is a typical example of the Scottish classical style which the three Adams, William the father, and Robert and James the sons, made so popular. I have not the date of its building, and apparently that most admirable work by McGibbon and Ross, entitled *Castellated and Domestic Architecture of Scotland*, was equally uncertain, for it states that the house was built "early in the present century"—meaning the nineteenth—by Lord Auchinleck. But Lord Auchinleck died in 1782 ; Robert Adam died in 1792 ; and Johnson's Boswell, the son of Lord Auchinleck, died in 1795. Grote's second volume, with the date 1797, but with notes on Auchinleck which were written before the death of James Boswell, says of the ruins of the old houses: "These at present belong to James Boswell, Esq., well known to the public by diverse ingenious publications. He resides in a handsome modern seat adjoining."

Samuel Johnson visited Auchinleck in 1773, and in his *Journey to the Western Islands of Scotland*, published in 1775, wrote: "Lord Auchinleck . . . has built a house of hewn stone, very stately and durable." Paterson, the author of *Ayrshire Families*, says that "he built the present mansion-house of the family." McGibbon and Ross state very precisely that the third house was that visited by

B

Dr. Johnson in 1773 ; and the *Ordnance Gazetteer of Scotland*, on page 85 of volume i., describes the modern house in these words, that it " is a good Grecian edifice built by Lord Auchinleck shortly before his death, and therefore is not the house where Johnson stayed in 1773."

From other statements it would seem that there has been a good deal of mere copying of a description of a " Grecian " house, without verification. The third house was added to the second, and Lord Auchinleck, who succeeded in 1748, probably added it soon afterwards. And it is quite reasonable to believe that he built the present house about 1780. I think that he planned it and began it, and that James Boswell the biographer finished it.

The mansion stands close to the banks of the River Lugar, which Burns mentions in the lines:

> " Behind yon hills where Lugar flows,
>   'Mang moors and mosses many, O,
> The wintry sun the day has closed,
>   An' I'll awa to Nannie, O."

It is in grounds which are beautifully wooded, lying between the glen of the Lugar and that of its tributary the Dippel, and including both streams. The long frontages are west and east, with the entrance in the east front. The approach is by a wooded avenue which reaches the house in a wide curve. The building is not excessively large, and is an oblong. But the front line on the east side receives an appearance of extension by subsidiary buildings at each end in the shape of curious towers quite detached from the house itself. There are two at each end.

The house comprises basement, ground floor, and upper floor, the basement only partly below the level of the ground. The stone-work of the basement is rustic ; the angles of the block are in the same style ; and the rest of the stone is ashlar.

The centre of the front is in the characteristic Adam style. A handsome flight of steps rises to the entrance, which is both a window and a door ; and the whole centre stands slightly forward from the line, with four fluted pilasters giving character to the design. The doorway is between the two middle pilasters, and Ionic capitals are a natural supplement. The entablature consists of a simple architrave and cornice with a plain frieze between them. Above is a pediment with a curved upper line, the tympanum being free from any design or carving. The entablature below the pediment of the four pilasters has a Latin inscription which struck me as being Horatian in its sentiment, and after a diligent search I found

AUCHINLECK
THE EAST FRONT

AUCHINLECK
THE LIBRARY

it in the Epistles, book i., epistle xi., to Bullatium. It is a line and a half, the last:

"QVOD PETIS, HIC EST,
EST VLVBRIS, ANIMVS SI TE NON DEFICIT ÆQVVS."

The meaning is: "What thou seekest, here it is, it is in Ulubræ, if contentment do not fail thee." Horace wrote the letter to a friend, Bullatius, who had the modern craze, the *wanderlust*, and had sought variety in Asiatic travel. The sentiment is practically, "there is no place like home," even if home be in a disagreeable and marshy place like Ulubræ, to the south-east of Rome.

The arrangement of the interior is simple and effective. The hall occupies the middle of the east front, the dining-room being immediately opposite the entrance, and the drawing-room entered from the right of the hall, with its chief feature a fine decorative ceiling of the Adam style. When I saw the house this room had an interesting painting of Sir Alexander Boswell, son of Johnson's biographer and the first baronet. A painting of old Lord Auchinleck hung in the dining-room. The library is a large room above the dining-room, and contained most of the books of the judge and the biographer, besides a collection of family portraits above the book-cases.

Recently a certain amount of excitement was caused by the sale of the contents of an "ebony cabinet" which used to be in Auchinleck House, and which contained many letters and papers of the biographer, especially the manuscript of the famous *Life of Samuel Johnson*. The papers, like many another collection, went to America. The box and its contents had been away from Scotland since Lord Talbot de Malahide, the great-great-grandson of James Boswell, removed them to his Irish seat when he sold Auchinleck a few years ago. It is a matter of real interest that the estate was sold to a Boswell, Lieutenant-Colonel John Douglas Boswell, who now lives in the Boswell house.

James Boswell gave a short sketch of the family history, the salient points in which are of interest and are easily recounted. Originally the lands were held by a family which took its name from them—"de Auchinleck," in those days pronounced "Affleck," which is a not uncommon Scottish name. In 1504 the family was forfeited, and the lands were given by King James IV. to Thomas Boswell, one of the Boswells of Balmuto in Fife. He was killed at Flodden in 1513, with his patron, but the lands went on through his descendants in the male line until a different entail enabled them to pass in the female line to Lord Malahide.

The first baronet inherited the literary tendencies of his father, and was a poet and a journalist, who also was a Member of Parliament. His journalism got him into trouble with James Stuart, of Dunearn, and they fought a duel, in which Stuart had the bad luck to shoot his opponent. But Sir Alexander had worse luck, for he died of his wound, and it was through his daughter that Lord Malahide succeeded.

Sir Alexander wrote both serious and humorous verse, one of his best-known poems being " Jenny Dang the Weaver," telling of how she dismissed her suitors :

> " Quo' he, ' My lass, to speak my mind
>   I troth I needna swither ;
> You've bonny een, and if you're kind
>   I'll never seek anither ;'
> He humm'd and haw'd, the lass cried ' Feugh !'
>   And bade the coof not deave her ;
> Syne snapt her fingers, lap and leugh,
>   And dang the silly weaver.
>
>   And Jenny dang, Jenny dang,
>   Jenny dang the weaver ;
>   Syne snapt her fingers, lap and leugh,
>   And dang the silly weaver."

BALCARRES HOUSE, COLINSBURGH, FIFE

THE country around Balcarres House is very picturesque, without wildness, and slopes upward to the hilly interior of Fife. The house stands where the ground has entered distinctly upon the rise, and the main avenue ascends steadily. It is long, and is entered by a gateway from the main road which runs across country from Largo to Pittenweem. The entrance is known by the romantic name of " The Golden Gate." It is a highly ornamental piece of ironwork, and has its name from the amount of gilding which decorates it.

The avenue arrives at the house on the north side, which presents an aspect of two great blocks at right angles to each other, the larger being the north wing. To the north extends a great park with rough grass and many trees; but the ground is clear close to the house, so that we are able to obtain an impressive and complete view of the building. The north front of the north block, three storeys in height, presents in line, from east to west, a crow-stepped gable projecting in front of the block, a round tower corbelled out from the first storey and carrying a conical roof, and another crow-stepped gable with a round tower on each side, corbelled out from a higher level. The last of these is at the north-west angle. This front contains windows which are mullioned and transomed.

The west front of this north block is divisible into two parts, the northern modern and the southern old. The latter part is plainer and has been altered. At its southern end another block projects west, and contains the principal entrance. The relation of the two blocks at right angles carries out the old Scottish plan, but deviates from it by the entrance being at the extremity instead of in the angle. The general characteristics on the west front are similar to those of the north, with pedimented dormer windows added.

The south front shows a much plainer exterior, divided into west and east sections. The western part has great bay windows on the ground and first floors, while at the east end a handsome flight of steps rises to a window, and has an open classical balustrade. This front introduces us to a remarkable feature of Balcarres House— its magnificent terrace gardens. The upper terrace extends to the east, where it rises by a few steps. Where the east end of the south front goes back to the north, a great yew hedge runs from north to south. To the south of the termination of the hedge is a fine example of garden architecture. A great central terrace stands high above the level of the other, square in form, and surrounded by a classical balustrade, supported on low columns set close together. The south side of the balustrade is opened to allow a broad flight of steps to descend. Having descended to about the level of the west upper terrace, it divides to west and east in two flights which go down to the south from a half-landing, and two opposite flights which descend to the north from the same half-landing. The lower terrace which is thus reached is very charmingly laid out. Between the two south flights is an arched alcove in the wall of the central terrace, in front of which is a long stone basin filled with water flowing from a fountain. On the west and east sides are stone seats in alcoves, the whole designed after the model of the strict classical manner. Closely trimmed yew-trees abound on the lowest terrace, and a wonderful maze of dwarf hedging of yew occupies a great space immediately to the south. This architectural garden is a magnificent sight, while the view from the upper terrace, taking in the Firth of Forth in the distance far beyond the grounds, is full of poetic charm.

The interior of the house is in keeping with its surroundings. From the entrance-hall a few steps to the left lead to the corridor. On the right is the library, while on the left we reach the panelled room, the breakfast-room, and the dining-room. A distinguishing feature of all the rooms is their ceilings, elaborately and beautifully moulded. The library has a very fine fireplace, with a canopy of oak made in the ancient shape. On the canopy is a coat of arms with supporters, all in the true heraldic colours. The date carved under the arms is 1759.

The ceiling of the panelled room is in blue and gold, the panelling being oak, and filled with carved figures drawn from scriptural and classical subjects. The drawing-room is comparatively small, very pretty; and the dining-room is large, with a handsome fireplace. At its east end, where the breakfast-room joins it, are two fine examples of the art of Romney.

The owner of this house is David Alexander Edward Lindsay, 27th Earl of Crawford and 10th Earl of Balcarres. He possesses an inheritance of intellectual ability as well as of position, and did remarkable service during the Great War. But the purpose of these chapters is to say little about the work of present owners, while relating what is interesting about families.

BALCARRES HOUSE
THE SOUTH FRONT

BALCARRES HOUSE
TERRACES TO THE SOUTH
OF THE HOUSE

BALCARRES HOUSE, FIFE

The family of Lindsay is one of the oldest and greatest in Scottish history, and the Earl of Crawford is the premier Earl of Scotland. Several of the name were known in England towards the close of the eleventh century, brought over by William the Conqueror. One of them, Baldric de Lindesay, has his name preserved in the chartulary of the monastery of St. Evreux in Normandy, to which he gave tithes in 1086 of the manors which he held of the Earl of Chester.

They were in Scotland soon afterwards, and Sir Walter de Lindesay followed David, youngest son of King Malcolm Canmore, when he took possession of the Principality of Cumberland. This David became King of Scotland in 1124. Sir Walter de Lindesay of Fordington, William who was perhaps his brother, and William's son Walter, all gave charters, especially to Dryburgh Abbey. William, son of Walter, sat in the Scottish Parliament in 1180 as Baron of Luffenach, which is Luffness in East Lothian. He married Alienora de Limesi, who may have belonged to the same family, as some say that "Lindesay" is a variation of that name. He is the direct ancestor of the present Earl.

One of the family was one of the regents of Scotland in 1255, and his son Alexander was a companion of Wallace and a supporter of Bruce. Sir Alexander's son David was Lord of Crawford and the Byres, Constable of Edinburgh Castle in 1346, and one of the signatories of the letter to Pope John XXII. asserting the Independence of Scotland. His third son, Sir Alexander, was father of David, the 1st Earl of Crawford, who was a mighty man of valour, born probably in 1359, and married to a daughter of King Robert II.

He accepted a challenge which the English Lord Welles offered to any Scottish Baron, and the duel was fought on London Bridge on the Feast of St. George in 1390. He performed two feats, jumping off his horse and back again in armour to show that his immovable seat was not artificial, and, after unhorsing Lord Welles, lifting him on his dagger point, and throwing him. Having thus dealt faithfully with his opponent, who survived the rough usage, he led him gently to the Queen and presented him. It was no disgrace to be beaten by such a warrior, and the English feasted the victor royally in their admiration.

His grandson, the 3rd Earl, had the misfortune to be killed in trying to prevent a fight between the Lindsays and the Ogilvys of Airlie, he having married an Ogilvy of Auchterhouse. He was under excommunication by James Kennedy, Bishop of St. Andrews, and no one would bury him until the excommunication was removed. His son Alexander, the 4th Earl, was known as " Earl

7

Beardie," and is said to be still playing cards with the devil in a secret chamber in the Castle of Glamis.

An extraordinary compact was made by Ludovic, the 16th Earl of Crawford, with John, the 1st Earl of Lindsay, who apparently had got the other into his power. Ludovic surrendered his earldom in favour of the heirs male of his body, after whom to the Earl of Lindsay, who was Lord Lindsay of the Byres. It was only on the death of the 22nd Earl that the title went again to the right line, then represented by Alexander, 6th Earl of Balcarres, whose son claimed in 1848 and was recognised. Alexander, the 25th Earl, was a distinguished author; and his son, the late Earl, was an equally distinguished astronomer and father of the present Earl, who is therefore the 27th.

III

BALCASKIE, PITTENWEEM, FIFE

PITTENWEEM is supposed to derive its name from a cave, or *wame*, which existed in 1710, when Sir Robert Sibbald wrote his famous *History of Fife*. There were two chambers in it, the upper approached by steps from the lower. Then a long passage led to the Abbey, with steps which gave entrance directly into the dining-hall, or refectory. Technically the ecclesiastical foundation was a Priory, but that does not matter much in the present connection, and is only mentioned to indicate the antiquity and interest of the neighbourhood. Pittenweem is about three miles east of the well-known summer resort of Elie; and Balcaskie is about two miles from Pittenweem on a road which runs to the north-west.

The house is reached by an avenue of considerable length, and is an oblong block of rectangular shape, with variations at the four corners. The dimensions are imposing, as the front presents a line of somewhere about 140 feet from east to west. It is an extension of an older mansion, the original shape of which is believed to have been similar to the present. Looking to the north front, in which is the principal entrance, it might be described as a rectangular block, with a square block added at each angle, a rectangular court cut out of the middle part of the north side, and a round tower at the west end to contain a stair.

The old house was described by Sibbald in these words—"A little above Pittenweem to the north-west is Balcaskie, a very pretty new house, with all modish conveniences of terraces, gardens, park, and planting. It was anciently the possession of lairds of the name of Strang, and is now the seat of Sir Robert Anstruther, brother to my Lord Anstruther." The builder of the house was Sir William Bruce, second son of Robert Bruce of Blairhall, descended from the family of Bruce of Clackmannan. He was architect to King Charles II., and completed the Palace of Holyroodhouse. He bought Balcaskie in 1665, and was created a baronet in 1668. He ultimately sold the property, having acquired others; and Sir Thomas Stewart purchased it in 1684. The building of the house may quite reasonably be assigned to about the year 1670.

9

Sir Ralph Abercromby Anstruther, grandfather of the present owner, filled in the spaces on the east and west sides between the square turrets. He added the present porch on the north front, constructed the balcony on the south side, and threw out the bow window in the south-west turret.

Unfortunately he did a bit of destructive work by removing a round stair tower which stood approximately at the north-west corner of the drawing-room, not quite at the middle of the west wall. He also made the interior stair from the hall to the billiard-room.

While the north front is the entrance front, the south front is more attractive, partly due to the architecture and partly to the open outlook upon beautiful gardens which face the south. Also on this side there is a delightful view over the Firth of Forth, with the Isle of May appearing at no great distance. The square turrets at the ends of the north front have their counterparts on this front. The unbroken outline is longer than on the north front, and the greater length is used to the advantage of the general appearance by the existence of a continuous balcony on the level of the first floor. Drawing-room, library, and dining-room all open on it.

The west end of the house presents a varied architectural appearance. Two square blocks at the angles, a crow-stepped gable in the middle, a round tower on each side of that part, a conical roof on one tower, and an ogee roof on the other, are the features.

In the interior, the porch leads to a large hall, from which on the left rises a stair, which leads to the billiard-room, a very interesting feature of the house. The billiard-room is really an upper corridor, of a form unusual in Scotland. The stair leads directly into it from below, not from a landing by a doorway. And the opening is guarded at the top by a handsome wooden balustrade. The room is long, and is full of interesting portraits, among them being paintings of Sir Ralph and Lady Anstruther, the present baronet and his wife, by Birley.

The south wall of the billiard-room divides it from the library and the drawing-room, which are entered from it. The dividing wall is so thick that the door into the library is doubled, while that into the drawing-room is in a deep recess; and the explanation is that the wall was the north outside wall of the house built in 1670. It even suggests an older house.

The ceilings are a great feature of all the principal rooms, as we might expect from Sir William Bruce being the builder. The drawing-room is one of Bruce's rooms, lighted by four windows, and looking out upon the south balcony. It contains a particularly

BALCASKIE
THE WEST END
AND THE SOUTH FRONT

BALCASKIE
A GARDEN TERRACE

handsome ceiling—an oblong framed in oblongs, with squares let into the main pattern at the corners. There is an oval centre of highly decorative design, and the long sides of the rectangular frame are broken by quite plain middle squares. The corner squares have a decoration of a single pendent bunch of grapes in each; and a similar decoration hangs from an eight-pointed star occupying the very centre of the plaster ceiling. The room is somewhere about 40 feet in length.

The library is a continuation to the east of the old part of the house, and can be entered from the drawing-room, although it has its own separate door from the billiard-room. The ceiling has an octagonal centre, painted, in which there is a female figure, probably a Venus, surrounded by Cupids. The rest of the ceiling is divided into octagons, with winged female figures occupying the remaining spaces.

The dining-room ceiling also is pictorial, and the walls are distinguished by the large number of family portraits, going back through the generations to the Anstruther who bought the house in 1698, and to his grandfather who died about 1640.

The name " Balcaskie " is said to mean the " Town of the Pasch," but the derivation is not very convincing. There is a charter which I have seen and read, given by Alexander II., and dated November 5, 1223, confirming to Juan Cook, son of Nigel Cook, the lands of Balcaskie, in the territory of Kelly. This family probably assumed the name of the lands, for we have Thomas de Balcaskie in 1221, and many others of the name afterwards. Thomas de Balcaskie was Rector of Culter in 1388, but by that time the lands were in other hands.

The next family which possessed Balcaskie was that of Strang. The property, however, appears to have been divided among portioners as late as 1620; and this gives countenance to the possibility that there existed a small strong house on the present site. John Strang of Balcaskie married Cecilia, daughter of Henry de Anstruther, before 1362, and in that year received from his father-in-law tenements in the neighbouring town of Anstruther. William Strang of Balcaskie had in 1450 a charter of one-quarter of Balcaskie. In 1449 John Strang and Mariota Moulterer, his spouse, had a charter of one-quarter of Reedie Myres, a portion of Balcaskie.

At a later date the proprietors were David Moncrieff and Sir Alexander his brother, who belonged to the family of Moncrieff of that ilk. David married the heiress of one of the portioners. After the Moncrieffs came Sir William Bruce; then Sir Thomas Stewart, son of Sir Thomas Stewart, of Grantully; and after him,

Sir George Nicolson, of Kennay. The present laird is the descendant of Sir Robert Anstruther who bought the lands in 1698; and he was the third son of Sir Philip Anstruther of Anstruther. Sir Robert had been created a baronet in 1694, and the lands and baronetcy have proceeded directly from father to son, with one break, when the son of General Robert Anstruther succeeded his grandfather.

General Anstruther had secured the retirement of Sir John Moore's army into Corunna after the battle in which Sir John was mortally wounded. But General Anstruther died in Corunna, and was buried beside his leader. The present baronet, sixth holder of the title, was a Captain in the Royal Engineers, and saw service in the Egyptian campaign of 1882 and in Bechuanaland in 1885.

IV

BEMERSYDE, MERTON, BERWICKSHIRE

BEMERSYDE, the seat of the late Field-Marshal Earl Haig, has had a glorious eminence since it became the gift of the nation to the great Commander who so splendidly upheld the honour of the Empire on the fields of Flanders. But in 1928 it reached a sad pre-eminence in the sudden call of the Field-Marshal from the scene of his earthly labours, and his burial within a short distance of his home makes the neighbourhood a place of pilgrimage and his tomb a sacred shrine.

There is a wonderful amount and variety of interest in the locality in which the old house stands. The parish is Merton, which forms a " salient "—expressive word, inheritance from the War—of southern Berwickshire jutting into the northern boundary of Roxburghshire. The salient is about four miles deep and of a mean width of about two miles. It is bounded on the west by the River Tweed, which is joined by the River Leader from the north. The river thus increased in volume has found itself up against the wall of rock which ordered the direction of the Leader, and it now proceeds towards the south, afterwards curving round and flowing eastward. Its southern course is full of great windings and loops, and it is in one of those loops that the lands of Bemersyde lie. Further within the loop are the remains of Dryburgh Abbey.

Almost due west across the river is the town of Melrose, four miles distant ; while at a distance of eight miles a little south of the same direction is the town of Selkirk. Close to Melrose, and well seen from Bemersyde, are the Eildon Hills, the conspicuous landmarks of that part of Southern Scotland. Further south and across the river, two and a half miles away is St. Boswells—the full and correct name of which is Newtown St. Boswells. Between St. Boswells and Dryburgh is a footbridge across the river from Roxburghshire to Berwickshire. From it on the Berwickshire side runs the Old Monks' Road ; and near Dryburgh is the colossal statue of Sir William Wallace which the 11th Earl of Buchan erected in 1814.

13

The great Roman station of Newstead, on the lands of Dry-grange and Ravenswood in the county of Roxburgh, are not far off. Reburied as the remains now are, the knowledge of the great station, so carefully and skilfully unearthed and described in the years from 1905 till 1911, when a full volume was published, remain. We know that Agricola's army marched up the Tweed and made the camp ; that other armies followed ; and that until near the end of the second century of our era Roman garrisons were either continuous or frequent.

During that time conflicts were many with the Celtic inhabitants —for Celtic they were, as is shown in the ornamentation of sword-hilts found among the Roman remains. A great collection of well over 2,000 articles from this station lies in the Museum of the Society of Antiquaries of Scotland in Edinburgh.

Roughly two centuries afterwards came the invasions of the Northmen. Up the valley of the Tweed they pursued their march ; and they did their work more completely than did the Romans, if the absence of Celtic place-names and the presence of Norse and Danish names is to be taken as good evidence. Thus in time arose the kingdom of Northumbria ; and then in further time the feuds of the Borders, so that the country between the Tweed and the Forth was always a country of warriors. In the midst of that country arose Bemersyde.

As a modern residence Bemersyde House stands on a rocky eminence overhanging the river, its principal and entrance front facing the south. It consists of a central part with wings to west and east. The central part is the most striking, as it is also the oldest, part of the building, rising at the present day to a height of four storeys. The wing on the right, that is, on the east end, is only two storeys high, while that on the west, the left of the whole front, contains two parts, that nearer the central block three storeys and that further away two storeys only.

The low part to the right gives the centre block the advantage of showing on its east end the very Scottish feature of a crow-stepped gable, but this must not be taken as the original form of that block. A look at the front of the block carries us further back in time than the crow-stepped gable period, and tells us of the time when such a house was built on the plan of a plain oblong, square or rectangle. The front wall shows us a doorway and five plain windows, evidently larger than the first windows, although they are not really large now. Topping the third storey is a plain parapet on corbels, with small bartizans at the angles. That was the original level of the roof, to which in time was doubtless added a capehouse. The cape-

BEMERSYDE
THE SOUTH FRONT

BEMERSYDE
AFTER J. M. W. TURNER, R.A.

house has given place to the present fourth storey, the front of which is somewhat behind the parapet, and the ends of which are finished as crow-stepped gables.

The great authority for the history of the house and its family is *The Haigs of Bemersyde*, by John Hunter, published in 1881. It describes the house as being seven centuries old, which would take it back to the twelfth century. That, however, must not be taken as an architectural estimate. There is evidence of great age in the vaulted ceilings of the lowest rooms ; but they do not prove the twelfth century, and all that can be said is that there was doubtless a house in existence in that century.

Sir Walter Scott loved the house, and took the greatest interest in it. He took the painter Turner to it in the year 1831, when Turner was making sketches to illustrate the edition of Sir Walter's poems which was published in 1833. In *Border Antiquities* Sir Walter wrote : " The style of architecture and defence employed here and at Bemerside Tower, four miles distant, is that pointed out by an Act of the Scottish Parliament in 1535, where, among other preparations for defending his kingdom, it was the policy of James V. to increase the number of strongholds upon the Borders, by compelling every proprietor of an £100 land of valuation to construct such a fortress as might be a place of refuge to his neighbours in case of invasion." The other place to which Scott referred was Smailholm Tower, a Border " peel " of the same style. They are both very similar to the oldest parts of many of the houses described in the present chapters. At the same time, Scott doubted if the Act was ever enforced. But the times, apart from any Act of Parliament, enforced the style. Hunter's and Scott's divergent dates may easily be reconciled—a stronghold was there from early times, and those old peels received addition and strengthening according to the danger of the period and the resources of the owners.

Hunter states that the upper portion was modified considerably about the year 1690 ; and that may be taken as the date of the crow-stepped fourth storey. In 1796 the low east wing was added. A wing, probably similar, was added on the west at a later date, and part of this was raised to a third storey in 1859. The late Field-Marshal made some alterations, and that practically completes the story of the growth of the house.

Turner's drawing remains as a most interesting picture of the house as Sir Walter Scott and he saw it in 1831, in the time of the laird who bore the name of James Zerubbabel Haig. In that sketch the group in front comprises Sir Walter Scott leaning on the arm of Lockhart, with Miss Haig near, while Turner is seen sketching in the distance. A portrait propped up on the ground is that of the laird. The party had lunched with the laird.

Often is quoted, sometimes not quite accurately, a couplet attributed to Thomas the Rhymer, whose place of Ercildoune is near:

> " Tyde what may betyde,
> Haig shall be Haig of Bemersyde."

And the couplet has remained true till the present day. Putting aside the traditional origins, which are probably fabulous—although we should like to believe that the family origin was Pictish—there is charter evidence of Petrus de Haga between 1150 and 1200. And then they went from father to son—another Petrus, Henricus, Petrus, Johannes, Petrus, and another Henricus. This last appears to have been succeeded by his brother Johannes ; and then again they went from father to son—Andrew, John, Gilbert, James, William, Robert, Andrew, Robert, and James, who was laird from 1602 till 1619, and from whom descended a line of lairds which ended six or seven generations later in a lady, Sophia Haig. At the same time a parallel line was descending from the same James of the year 1602 through his second son Robert of St. Ninian's, perhaps senior to that in possession, and Robert's line sent out branches, to one of which the late Field-Marshal belonged. When Sophia died, Bemersyde went to Lieutenant-Colonel Arthur Balfour Haig of that line, reached by about six generations up the line and then eight generations down, so that the connection was very distant indeed. It was from him that the estate was purchased in 1921, to be made the gift of the nation to Field-Marshal Earl Haig.

The Haigs of Bemersyde, the Erskines of Shieldfield, and the Halliburtons of Merton, have had for centuries the right of burial in the precincts of Dryburgh Abbey, in return for great gifts which they made to the foundation. The first Petrus de Haga, Laird of Bemersyde, gave Flatwood and Threepwood. That is the reason why the Abbey is Earl Haig's resting-place. And next to it is that of Sir Walter Scott, whose great-grandfather James Haliburton married Margaret Haig.

V

BIEL, PRESTONKIRK, EAST LOTHIAN

BIEL HOUSE stands less than three miles away from Dunbar in East Lothian. It is " the fortalice of Biel " of very ancient documents, but is very different now from the old fortalice, as the result of many extensions. Probably the site was just wide enough for the old fortalice—a square tower. There is no doubt that much of the old building is embodied in the present house, perhaps even part of the very first walls. The site overhangs the Biel Burn; and the extensions, which have been very great, have gone both east and west and have made a very long building. The entrance front faces the north; and a Gothic arch, forming a gateway without a gate, stands at right angles to it on our left as we face that front. At a short distance is a handsome ivy-covered Gothic porch, above which is a coat of arms with supporters. The part of the house between this and the Gothic arch, under which the avenue runs, is two storeys in height, with plain square-headed windows and some Gothic-shaped narrow windows.

To the west the wall of the house is higher than the part on the east, and battlemented. To the right rises a square tower behind the front of the house, the right being west. Further to the right there is great variation of form; but the three-storeyed section of the front, the great square tower with a slender octagonal turret fronting it, and some neighbouring interior walls, form the oldest parts. The lower part of the square tower contains the original walls of the fourteenth-century building, as is shown by the vaulted interiors of the basement.

The extreme left was built by William Hamilton Nisbet before 1820; while a part to the west or right was built by the late Mrs. Nisbet Hamilton Ogilvy and contains the chapel, of which no part has a share in the north front.

The southern front is even more impressive than the north, partly due to its own features, and partly because it has the advantage of three beautiful terraces below it and a " haugh," or meadow, extending from the base of the lowest terrace to the stream. If we look from the meadow, the length and height of the house both seem great. The most beautiful view is obtained from a considerable distance on the opposite bank of the Biel Burn through an opening in the trees. The three sections are there easily distinguished—the oldest in the middle, with the first Lord Belhaven's arms high up on the wall between two Gothic windows of the great tower; the most recent addition on the left, showing the handsome windows of the chapel; and the early nineteenth-century portion on the right. The general character is similar to that of the north front, but lighter and freer in treatment; and the drawing-room window, which springs out from the wall to the right of the great tower, is reached by a balcony from the terrace below.

The terraces are charmingly laid out with plants, shrubs, and flowers. They were originally laid out by the first Lord Belhaven, who was a strong loyalist of the time of Charles I. After the final defeat of the King, Belhaven fled across the Solway disguised as a labourer. He ultimately went to Kew, where he found work as a highly skilled Scottish gardener. He was employed to buy bulbs in Holland, and took the opportunity to convey letters to Charles II. A fine stone bridge over the stream still bears his arms and name.

There was, till recently, a memorial of the second Lord Belhaven on the south lawn, consisting of a grand cedar of Lebanon. The spread was 107 feet; and the circumference of the trunk at 5 feet from the ground was 21 feet 10½ inches. But during the severe gale of November 5, 1926, a succession of fierce blasts wrecked it before the eyes of the Laird of Biel. Lord Belhaven brought it in a pot from London. That Lord Belhaven was a strong opponent of the Act of Union, and on the wall of the house is an inscription which he placed there—" Traditionis Scotiae anno primo, 1707 ": *in the first year of the betrayal of Scotland.* In the wall of one of the terraces is an interesting stone chair which was brought from Athens about 1801 by Mrs. Hamilton Nisbet, mother of the Countess of Elgin, whose husband brought home the " Elgin Marbles."

The interior is worthy of the grand appearance of the exterior. One of the striking features is " The Corridor," a very long room running west from the entrance to the great staircase. The passage-way through the length of the house is continued beyond the staircase in a series of windings to the newest part.

South of the corridor and parallel with it is a series of seven rooms in line, so that it is possible to pass from east to west through all those rooms without entering a passage. Five of them are of fine proportions and are attractively decorated. The drawing-room is the finest of all the rooms, and has its charm enhanced by the fact that doors open from it on the west to the " White Room " and on the east to the " Ante-Drawing-Room," from which steps

BIEL HOUSE
THE ENTRANCE FRONT
FROM THE NORTH-EAST

BIEL HOUSE
THE TERRACED
SOUTH FRONT

lead down to the terrace. The " White Room " is panelled, and has on the walls handsome pieces of tapestry worked by the daughters of the second Duke of Rutland. There was a wealth of interesting objects, among them paintings and marbles, at one time.

One of the walks in the grounds is known as " The Lady's Walk," and it enshrines a story, that of " The White Lady of Biel," whose apparition has been seen. She was Anne Bruce of Earlshall, in Fife, a daughter of Andrew Bruce, younger of Earlshall. She married the third Lord Belhaven, but he turned out an unfaithful husband. He was a representative peer of Scotland in 1715, was appointed Governor of Barbados in 1721, and died on November 17, 1721, on his passage out. This is history, and it is verified that the ship foundered off the Scilly Isles, all on board being drowned.

Now comes tradition. It is said that Lady Belhaven was very beautiful, and that on account of her complexion she received the name of " The White Lady." " Wine shone through her throat," says the tradition; but the late Mrs. N. Hamilton Ogilvy told me that that is also said of Philippina Welser of Augsburg, a famous German beauty.

In 1777 the Belhaven title went in the male line, but the Biel estate passed to Mary Hamilton of Pencaitland, who married William Nisbet of Dirleton. Their eldest son married Mary, eldest daughter of Lord Robert Manners of Bloxholm; and the only child of this marriage was Mary, who married the 7th Earl of Elgin. The late Lady of Biel was a granddaughter of the Countess of Elgin through the eldest daughter, the Lady Mary Bruce, who became Lady Mary Christopher Nisbet Hamilton. Lady Mary's younger sister, Lady Lucy Bruce, married John Grant of Kilgraston, elder brother of Sir Francis Grant, President of the Royal Academy, and of General Sir Hope Grant, who served with distinction in the Indian Mutiny, the Sikh Wars, and in China. The son of Lady Lucy's son is the present Laird of Biel, Lieutenant-Colonel J. P. Nisbet Hamilton Grant, D.S.O., of Dirleton and Belhaven.

The grounds of Biel House contain some most interesting trees. A still finer specimen of the cedar of Lebanon than that which the gale overthrew is yet intact, and there is one of its relatives, the *Cedrus atlantica*. The cork tree, *Quercus suber*, is as much at home as in its native soil. Adjoining some magnificent beeches, including a specially fine copper beech, are to be seen *Cryptomeria japonica*, *Cratægus tanacetifolia*, the gingko, *Quercus ilex acutifolia*, while *Althea fratrex*, *Romneya Coulteri*, *Aloysia citriodora*, and *Sephora tetraptera*, the New Zealand laburnum, shelter themselves under the sunny walls.

Although the fine collection of pictures was dispersed in 1921, there remain a few of notable interest. The marble chair was the seat on which the Gymnasiarch sat, long before the Christian era, and was the gift of the Archbishop of Athens. It has bas-reliefs of the sacred olive, the vase of consecrated oil, the owl of Minerva, and the four-legged agonistic table on which the prizes lay. Until it was given to Mrs. Hamilton Nisbet it had stood in the Court of the Catholicon.

VI

BINNS, ABERCORN, LINLITHGOWSHIRE

BINNS is more commonly called " The Binns " in its own county. Abercorn is the parish, on the south side of the Firth of Forth, and Binns is one of its historic houses, probably its oldest creation, for it was built in 1623 by Thomas Dalyell, father of the famous General Thomas Dalyell. It is the property of a descendant of the General, Major Sir James Bruce Wilkie Dalyell, Bart., of Binns. It has received alterations and additions at various times, and in particular about the year 1820, when the fifth baronet probably gave it the complete form which it has today.

The modern entrance faces the north and is approached by an avenue. In front the ground is comparatively level, with a wide and open view to the north in which Blackness Castle, the vessels passing up and down the Firth, and the hills of Fife, stand out clearly. Binns Hill rises to the east of the house, very near it, clothed with trees to the summit, on which stands a tower.

The north front is three storeys in height, with a short extension at the west end of the line, only two storeys high. Two round towers in the front are four storeys in height, and divide the front into three sections, of which the two ends are similar and symmetrical. The general style is a combination of the Scottish baronial with the domestic Gothic; and the whole building is impressive by its size and its proportions. The corbelling beneath the crenellated parapets is extremely graceful and refined. The walls are plastered roughcast, so that changes in the stonework cannot be observed, but there is no difficulty about the age of this front as the interior bears it, 1630.

All the windows on this front are rectangular and of quite modern size, those on the upper floors having a moulding in the usual Jacobean style. The round towers have long slit windows, cross-shaped.

The west front presents a great deal of variety, with a length of outline, and reminds one rather of an English house of Tudor age than Scottish. The west end of the north front forms the northern part of the west front. The west line then falls back considerably

21

to the east towards the interior of the structure. Further south it again projects, thus forming a three-sided space.

The south front is low—merely one storey with highly ornate dormer windows of varied pediments with finials. Its approaches are peculiar. It has in front an inner court, but farther away is an outer court, lower than the inner and higher than the ground outside, so that both courts are reached by steps. The lower steps are approached by a sunk road, the ground on each side rising as if it were part of a defensive scheme. There are many interesting features here, one of them being a doorway which is just outside the inner court. Four heavy steps lead up to it, and above it is a pediment in the tympanum of which are the letters T and D, with a heart between them, doubtless the initials of the Thomas Dalyell who built the house, and standing out with beautiful distinctness today. The general impression obtained is that this south front may have been the first entrance front.

The modern entrance in the north front is without a separate porch, and leads into a large hall, stone-flagged, the plain white ceiling carried on an interior structure of flat arches on three sides, which give an arcade to the room. There is a handsome stone fireplace in the east wall, at one time painted, but now showing the stonework in its natural beauty. To the right at the back a passage leads to the dining-room; and, carrying on further, we reach a stair in one of the towers. Stairs, passages, and rooms in out-of-the-way places are characteristic, and many of the rooms have historical associations, or are interesting in themselves, such as the " Blue Room " and the " Sea Room," from the latter of which an excellent view of the sea is obtained.

There are discrepancies among writers upon Binns as to the dates of the building of the house and of the General's birth; but the family testimony is that the General was born in 1599, and that his father, Thomas Dalyell, bought the estate in 1612 from Sir William Livingston, of Kilsyth, although the transaction was not final until about thirty years later. Meanwhile he was doubtless building the house, for on a stone above the window of the Sea Room is the date 1621, while a panel of the drawing-room ceiling has a monogram made up of the letters T.D.J.B., standing for Thomas Dalyell and Jonet Bruce, with the date 1630. The latter date indicates that the house was not finished before that date, in which a beautiful ceiling was put up.

The Dalyells or Dalzells take the name from the barony of Dalziel in Lanarkshire, now the property of Lord Hamilton of Dalziel. The pronunciation in any of the three forms is the same—

THE BINNS
THE EAST AND
THE NORTH FRONTS

THE BINNS
THE OLD DOORWAY IN THE COURTYARD

as if " Dee-yell," with the second syllable accented. They were known in Scottish history as early as the thirteenth century. The family acquired Carnwath in the sixteenth century, and Sir Robert Dalzell, already Lord Dalzell in 1628, became Earl of Carnwath in 1639. Their old style was " of Dalzell and Elliok," and Thomas Dalyell, the first of Binns, is said to have been the grandson of John, son of Robert Dalzell of Dalzell and Elliok. Although Balfour Paul's *Scots Peerage*, while stating this, gives it as uncertain, the Binns family has always founded on the Carnwath family tree.

John Dalyell, like many Scottish younger sons, took to trade, was a merchant in Edinburgh, and doubtless made money. Probably Thomas did likewise. His wife was Jonet Bruce, whom he married in Edinburgh on December 8, 1601. The date on his tomb is 1642.

The terrible General succeeded in that year, but he cannot have done any building for a long time yet. He was on service for the King, and ultimately had to escape to the Continent, where he remained until 1665. In 1638, to avoid forfeiture, he made over his estates to his brother-in-law, William Drummond, of Riccarton, whose son Thomas duly handed them back to him in 1667. There are two paintings of the General in the house, one with the beard which is associated with his vow, and the other without it. The vow is said to have been made on the death of Charles I., that Dalyell would not shave until the royal line should be restored. The bearded picture is in the Blue Room, and the other in the dining-room.

The marble fireplace of the drawing-room has the royal arms over it, according to the custom by which Scottish families often testified their loyalty. The ceiling was evidently the work of a company of Italian artists who did the same work in various houses of the period—Holyrood, Winton, Auchterhouse, and others.

The Sea Room, a bedroom which looks out on the Firth from the top floor of the east end of the north front, has a ceiling worked by the same artists. It has the added distinction of being arched instead of flat, and its forms are not identical with those of the drawing-room.

The vaulted rooms in the basement have an interest all their own, partly architectural and partly legendary. A great deal of deduction has to be made from the legendary tales which have been handed down about the General. The fundamental fact is that he was an intense royalist, a soldier who fought for Charles I. and Charles II. in the three countries of the Union, captured at Worcester and immured in the Tower, from which he escaped in 1652. He was excluded by Cromwell from the Act of Grace and took service with the Czar of Russia.

Popular story said that he learned to roast prisoners in Russia, and that he applied the treatment to Covenanters in the vaulted kitchens of his great house of Binns. Bishop Burnet, who was rather an acrid historian, has some responsibility in this matter, although he only records that Dalyell "threatened to spit men and to roast them." The General made rather a curious entail of his lands, beginning with his eldest son's eldest son, and the heirs male, followed by the heirs female, of that grandson, before the other children of the General could come into the succession. The patent of baronetcy which was given to the General's son followed the entail, so that title and estates have gone three times through the female line.

VII

BLAIR, DALRY, AYRSHIRE

BLAIR is a house and an estate in the parish of Dalry and the County of Ayr which is a most remarkable example of growth from generation to generation. The outline of Blair is a capital **T**, with the horizontal line much longer than the vertical, which points almost due north—it has a deviation of perhaps twelve degrees to the east. The length of that top line is not far short of 200 feet, and represents probably four or five periods in the building of the whole. The upright line measures about 80 feet from its junction with the other line. The oldest part of the building is to be found on the east side of the upright line and the south side of the horizontal line, where the two sides form an angle. The buildings about that angle are really the nucleus of the whole edifice; and when we look at them we are absolutely certain that we see a definite part of what Timothy Pont, writing before 1604, described as the " ancient castell and strong dominion."

If we call the cross line the north block and the upright line the south block, that will locate an angle which is worthy of detailed mention. It contains two remarkable doorways, that on our left in present use, and the other an old doorway. Both are remarkable for their decoration and for the dates which are above them. That in present use has had a pediment, of which only the decorated face—the tympanum—remains. It has elaborate curvilinear carving in high relief surrounding a shield with two coats impaled—the dexter side that of Blair of Blair, and the other that of Hamilton, the whole shield representing William Blair and his wife Lady Margaret Hamilton, daughter of the second Duke of Hamilton. William Blair was retoured heir to his father in 1664. Above these heraldic emblems is a panel with the arms of Blair of Blair, a St. Andrew's Cross on which are nine lozenges, with a capital B on each side—a saltier between two letters B in fess. On the panel, in raised figures, is the date 1203.

Just above the other doorway the carvings are contained in three compartments in line, and the middle compartment contains in very plain figures the date 1617. The left compartment has the arms of Blair, but with only five lozenges with the letters; the compartment on the right contains those of Wallace of Craigie and the letters A.W. With the date, these indicate Bryce Blair and Annabel Wallace. Still higher up there is inset in the wall a very old stone with Gothic lettering, while two or three feet below, and just above the arms, is a plain stone of the same appearance. The lettering is " Sir Roger de Blair and Mary Muir his spouse." Her sister married King Robert II., and Sir Roger, who was a steady adherent of King Robert Bruce, died in 1329. The stones had evidently at one time formed a memorial niche enclosing an effigy in a church; but they and the dates do little to elucidate the dates of the house, although they are interesting as bringing together the names of old and eminent Ayrshire families, as were the Blairs and Mures. Possibly when Bryce Blair did some building or altering in 1617 he built into the wall stones discarded from the church by the zealots of the Reformation.

The part of the house under consideration is four storeys in height, with many crow-stepped gables and dormer windows. There is in it a fine vaulted room with very thick walls, and it forms the eastern termination of the oldest part.

A view of the whole north side of the cross line is interesting. There is a narrow terrace running the whole length, supported by a wall, from which the ground slopes rapidly and deeply to the bed of the Bombo Burn. As seen from the bed, the side rises most impressively, and the first castle must have been a place of some strength on that side.

On entering the house by the doorway in the oldest part, that under the date 1203, a vestibule gives access to the south part. This part, as originally added, was a separate building, to pass into which from any other part it was necessary to cross the open to a doorway in the adjoining wall. The date when this inconvenience ceased was 1850, when the present laird's father cut a passage through the solid wall of the old castle. A distance of 12 feet had to be cut through solid masonry, and the result is a passage from the north wall of the north block right along the east side of the south block. The 12-feet thick wall was the outside wall of the old keep, and is evidence of great age. McGibbon and Ross's great work on Scottish baronial architecture suggests 1400 as the date instead of 1203; and, if an equally good and equally unprovable conjecture may be allowed here, an almost indecipherable " 1393 " may have been copied as " 1203," assuming that 1203 is too early.

The passage slopes down to a most charming vaulted room now turned into a writing-room. It is a pity that the vaulted ceiling has been plastered; the original bare stonework would be so attrac-

BLAIR
THE OLDEST PART, LOOKING NORTH-WEST

BLAIR
THE TWO DOORWAYS IN THE SOUTH-EAST ANGLE

tive, as in " The Inch," a house to be noticed in a later chapter. The vaulting has a very wide span, with walls 6 feet thick at the base. And as the windows are cut in the thickness of the curve, it is clear that that part was built with a view to strength. The fireplace at the end is a feature in itself, although it is modern, in the old position and occupying the same space. A room near, also vaulted, and known as the " guard-room," was probably the old kitchen.

The drawing-room, on the first floor, with entrance cut in a thick wall which must have once been an outside wall of an addition to the original keep, extends the whole length of the upright line of the T, and is a room of magnificent proportions, about 65 feet long. It has a beautifully moulded plaster ceiling, very much in the style of some of those in Winton House. The room is divided into two parts by two pairs of tall fluted columns supporting a wide beam which carries the weight of the ceiling.

Across the landing from the drawing-room is the dining-room, which looks out to the north across the Bombo Burn. A long painting on the east wall is of antiquarian interest, as it depicts " The Last of the Leith Races." The date must be 1815, for those famous races were transferred to Musselburgh in 1816. When they originated is not known; but they were an old institution when the Duke of York, afterwards James VII., resided at Holyrood as Royal Commissioner in 1679. James Grant's description of the races, in his *Old and New Edinburgh*, from the records of eye-witnesses, pictures the meeting as a carnival, reaching its highest pitch of enjoyment on Saturday night, when " there was invariably a general brawl, a promiscuous free fight being maintained by the returning crowds along the entire length of Leith Walk."

Almost every room has its interest, four of them of special interest indicated by their names—the Italian room, the Napoleon room, the Buhl room, and the Dutch parquetry room. The Italian room is entirely furnished in the Italian style; the Napoleon room has a painting of the Emperor above the fireplace, and all its other pictures are associated with him; and in the Buhl room every article of furniture is of the type indicated by the name. Buhl is a kind of marquetry invented by a Frenchman, Charles André Boulle, who lived from 1642 till 1732. Its chief features are the inlaying of tortoise-shell, brass, and rosewood. Boulle used these materials with the instinct of an artist, so that time enhances the beauty and reputation of the style in spite of the competition of other styles. The bed in this room is a choice work of the artist.

The story of the Lairds of Blair would take a long time to write and much space, so a reference to the latest and to the earliest known must suffice here. The present Laird is Frederick Gordon Blair, C.B., C.M.G., late Lieutenant-Colonel and honorary Colonel commanding the Leicestershire Imperial Yeomanry. He saw much service in South Africa and in the Great War, and was A.D.C. to the King from 1914 to 1920.

The first of the family of whom there is record was William de Blair, mentioned in a contract between Ralph de Eglinton and the town of Irvine in 1205—this according to Paterson's *Ayrshire Families*.

VIII

BLAIRQUHAN, STRAITON, AYRSHIRE

STRAITON is only a little, quaint, and quiet village, with that charm which is to be found in out-of-the-way places. It has a church with all the characteristic ugliness of the buildings of the Scottish Reformation, but redeemed from complete condemnation by a pre-Reformation east end. And less than two miles from the village is the delightful house Blairquhan—pronounced " Blairwhon," with the accent on the second syllable, as nearly as spelling will indicate—a real modern castle, with a bit of the ancient castle embodied in it.

Blairquhan is finely situated on the banks of the River Girvan, the house being on the left bank and the river flowing through the grounds. The main frontage faces the south, with the ground rising from the front, and falling from the back of the house to the river, which winds its course for about four miles before it leaves the demesne. The avenue is entered by a handsome bridge and lodge, and is conducted along the river-bank a distance of nearly three miles before it arrives at the house. This gives the visitor a most pleasing impression. As the avenue draws near the house it passes under a row of lime-trees, old and lofty and dark.

The present house was built about the year 1820 by Sir David Hunter-Blair, Baronet, who was Deputy-Lieutenant and Convener of the County of Ayr; and the architect was William Burn, of Edinburgh. The former house was an irregular building of large extent, a great part of it erected in the reign of Mary Queen of Scots, about the year 1570. It was a total ruin at the time when it was taken down to make room for the present edifice, the only part which had withstood the ravages of time being a square tower of great strength and thickness, the " McQuirter Tower." Doubtless it was the original keep, erected for defence, and surviving when the additions which had been made for comfort had crumbled into pieces. The name of the tower was a record that the family of McQuirter had been connected in very early days with Blairquhan.

The front of the present house measures about 160 feet in line. A handsome porch stands out 24 feet in front of the line. At the east end is a series of low buildings surrounding the kitchen court-

29

yard, and containing a part of the old house which was rebuilt. Its most interesting feature is the beautifully arched old gateway, with a finely carved coat-of-arms above it. The inscription on the court gate contains the motto *In Domino confido*, and the statement, " At this tyme is Jone Kenedy Lard of Blarquhain, and Margret Keith his vyfe in the year of . . ." (probably about 1570).

The main entrance-hall, known as " The Saloon," is about 60 feet in height. A beautiful staircase rises from it, dividing at a half-landing, and continued as two staircases to a gallery from which passages communicate with all parts of the house, and upon which open various rooms.

The billiard-room opens from the left of the saloon; a little further on we come to the drawing-room on the left; and a wide doorway connects billiard-room and drawing-room, the former looking out to the south and the latter to the north and west. On the opposite side of the saloon are the dining-room and the library, running towards the east end of the house, which communicates with the ancient buildings.

As viewed on the south front the building is two storeys in height, but the slope down to the river on the north side gives another storey there. A rustic bridge where the River Girvan presents the appearance of a quiet pool makes a typical sylvan scene.

Of the families which have held Blairquhan, four are well known by name—MacWhirter, Kennedy, Whitefoord, and Hunter-Blair. An interesting tale tells of the passing of the estate from the MacWhirters and is the theme of a poem. Put in ordinary prose, it is written in a paper dated January 20, 1820, which was prepared for Sir David Hunter-Blair of that day.

The document reads: " Regnault Macwhurter, the last of the old race of the Macwhurters of Blairquhan, had twin daughters, one of whom was married to Sir Ulrich Macwhurter, who had been long in the service of the French king, and had been knighted by that prince for some valorous action. The other was joined in wedlock to a son of John, second Lord Kennedy, by his second wife Elizabeth Gordon, daughter of the Earl of Huntly. Upon the death of old Macwhurter these two gentlemen claimed the barony of Blairquhan, each for himself on account, as both said, of his lady having been born first. As this circumstance could not by any means be determined, a bloody foray would in all probability have ensued had not the relations on each side prevailed upon them to submit their claims to the King, James III., who although very young, had the character of being a wise and just prince.

" After much hesitation and many a stipulation they both agreed

BLAIRQUHAN
THE MAIN FRONT
FROM THE SOUTH

BLAIRQUHAN
THE MAIN STAIRCASE

to do so, and for that purpose proceeded to Edinburgh; but how to decide impartially a question where both parties seemed to have an equal right His Majesty was for some time at a loss to know. At last he came to the resolution that one of them should walk and the other ride from Edinburgh to Blairquhan, and he who should first kindle a fire in the castle should keep possession, not only of it, but likewise of all the land appertaining thereto; and to make the chance equal they were to draw each a straw out of a stack, and he who should pull the longest should ride. This fell to young Kennedy, who was consequently considered by many as having already gained the estate; but others, who knew Sir Ulrich's great strength and unbending resolution, were of a contrary opinion.

" There being no public road at that time from Edinburgh direct to Blairquhan, each took the route which fancy pointed out as being the straightest. Sir Ulrich was attended by many of the relations of young Kennedy on horseback, who were deputed by the King to see him perform his journey in the manner prescribed. Young Kennedy was not accompanied by any person, as none would undertake to ride as fast as he was likely to do; but he was preceded by His Majesty and a few nobles who wished to be at Blairquhan before either of the sticklers for the estate should arrive, in order that they might act as stewards of the race."

" But just as the King was going to cross the water of Girvan near Straiton, from that circumstance called the King's Hill to this day, he observed a great smoke suddenly arise from the highest chimney of the castle of Blairquhan, and being certain it could not be Kennedy that had raised it, as he was at that moment still a few yards in the rear of His Majesty's company, he exclaimed, ' My kingdom to a bodle that yon reek is raised either by the deil or by his ain bairn, Ulrich Macwhurter.' "

This is only about half of the account. Macwhurter obtained the award, but became such a terror to the neighbourhood that in course of time means were taken to get rid of him, and young Kennedy then came into the estate. The story is open to criticism but may be true, although it is known that John Kennedy was in possession in 1444, while James III. reigned between 1460 and 1488.

The estate passed to the Whitefoords in 1623, by a legal process which the Kennedys resisted, keeping possession for many years against the law. The Whitefoords held until Sir John was ruined by his connection with the Douglas and Heron Bank, after which the curators of Sir David Hunter-Blair bought the property about the end of the seventeenth century. The present laird is Captain Edward Hunter-Blair, R.N. He retired from the Royal Navy in 1898, but rejoined in 1914 and served at the naval centres of intelligence during the war, at Invergordon, Sheerness, and Greenock. The baronet is his elder brother Sir David Oswald Hunter-Blair, formerly Abbot of the Benedictine Monastery at Fort Augustus. The family is descended from the Hunters of Hunterston and the Blairs of Dunskey, and through the latter family, also from the Kennedys who held Blairquhan long ago.

IX

BONALY TOWER, COLINTON, MIDLOTHIAN

THE famous Scottish judge, Lord Cockburn, made Bonaly Tower a place of interest on account of his own personality and of the legal and literary associations which he accumulated around it. He also gave it the architectural features which make it worthy of notice as a building. In his day it was famous as the resort of the legal stars of the period, and that house entertained the social and literary celebrities of Edinburgh in that city's palmiest days to an extent which cannot be surpassed by any existing house.

The house, of which the name is pronounced "Bon-ale-y," with the accent on the middle syllable, stands in one of the most romantic and attractive situations which could possibly have been chosen, a little to the south of the village of Colinton and at the base of the Pentland Hills. At one time Bonaly was a village, with works, but in 1811 there appears to have remained only a dilapidated farmhouse, with odd ruins of cottages. Cockburn first removed those odd buildings, and then set himself to improve the house, which possibly was respectably old. Long afterwards, in his *Memorials of his Time*, he wrote: " In March, 1811, I married, and set up my rural household gods at Bonaly, in the parish of Colinton, close by the northern base of the Pentland Hills; and, unless some avenging angel shall expel me, I shall never leave that paradise. I began by an annual lease of a few square yards and a scarcely habitable farmhouse. But realising the profanation of Auburn, I have destroyed a village and erected a tower, and reached the dignity of a twenty-acred laird. Everything except the two burns, the few old trees, and the mountains, are my own work, and to a great extent the work of my own hands."

Henry Cockburn bought the property from Gillespie's Hospital, his first association with it being merely that of taking the house and some ground as a feu—a Scottish term for an everlasting lease subject to the payment of the annual rent, which is known as the " feu duty." Gillespie's Hospital had been founded by James Gillespie of Spylaw, near Colinton, one of two brothers, of whom the other was John, who appear in Kay's *Portraits*. James made money by grinding snuff at a mill which he had put up at Spylaw. Ultimately he kept a carriage, for which the celebrated wit, Henry Erskine, suggested as a motto :

> " Wha wad hae thocht it,
> That noses had bocht it."

James bought the lands of Spylaw and Fernielaw in 1773, died on April 8, 1797, was buried in Colinton Churchyard, and left his estate and £12,000 for the founding of a hospital " for the aliment and maintenance of old men and women." Henry Cockburn was the next owner of Bonaly.

To have an idea of the house as it passed into Henry Cockburn's hands we must go to what is now the back. The Bonaly Burn runs there close to the house, on the north side of the building, where a footbridge crosses the Burn at the north-west corner. An immense tree stands beside the footbridge, so that very little is seen of the building; but what is seen is the old and original wall, on which has been erected a third storey, and the present back of the house was formerly the front.

Whatever alterations he may have made at first, the prominent feature which is associated with his name is the great square tower, which gives to the whole structure a mediæval aspect. And that certainly makes it a notable house from the architectural point of view. Lord Cockburn died in 1854, and in the same year his trustees sold the estate to John Gray the publisher; and it was he, not Cockburn, who added the third storey to the original two of the farmhouse. Gray sold the place to W. T. Thomson, manager of the Standard Insurance Company, in 1866. Although Gray's tenure was short, he introduced gas into the house. Thomson's tenure was still shorter, for he sold the property in 1874 to Professor W. B. Hodgson, the first Professor of Political Economy in the University of Edinburgh. Professor Hodgson made the greatest alteration since Cockburn's time, by adding to the south, at the west end of the south front, an additional block, which contains the library. After the death of Professor Hodgson's widow, the trustees sold the estate to David Simson, of the Colonial Service, in 1889. His widow occupied the house until her death in 1918, and Andrew Glegg, W.S., bought it in 1919. He sold it in a few years, and it is now the property of Mrs. Ogilvie.

Bonaly is approached from Colinton by a road which slopes up the gentle declivity of the base of the Pentland Hills. A gateway gives entrance to an avenue which reaches the house from the

BONALY TOWER
FROM THE SOUTH-WEST

BONALY TOWER
THE SOUTH FRONT

east. A beautiful lawn extends in front and well to the east. As it stands now, the great square keep is the outstanding feature, with a wall leading away to the east and enclosing a yard. Just where this wall joins the keep rises a staircase which forms the main entrance to the house. This part does not seem to have suffered any alteration of design since the judge's time.

The keep has no windows in the east wall, and has its angles rounded. In the angle formed on the south by the peel and the addition of Hodgson rises a round tower, which contains a secondary entrance, and rises considerably above the level of the square tower, with a doorway giving on to the roof of the tower. The view from the top is said to embrace the counties of Perth, Stirling, Clackmannan, Kinross, Fife, and the three Lothians; but no part of the view is more enthralling than the magnificent outline of the Pentland slopes as they stretch away to east and west.

Lord Cockburn's Bowling Green, famous in references to the judge's hospitality, stands to the west of the house, well surrounded by trees. Around the bowling green are various sculptured stones, standing today as they were placed by Henry Cockburn himself. One of them is a curious sundial, dismounted from its pedestal, and placed on another old stone. It is a cube surmounted by a cherub head with outspread wings. On the visible faces is the inscription, " A. McMY1733," but nothing to indicate the place of origin. Not far from this is a full-size statue of Shakespeare.

But away to the south-east of the house probably the most curious stones used to stand near a gate in a rough stone setting, perhaps the remains of an old building, and open in front, overhung by trees and covered with climbing foliage. At each end of the open front was a full-covered figure under an inscribed arch. One represents King Robert Bruce in full armour, and the other is believed to be " the good Sir James " Douglas. They now form the gateway to the flower garden, and are supposed to have been brought from Linlithgow Palace or Stirling Castle; but there is no record as to the places whence were carried the other stones. The days were those of the Vandals, of whom Cockburn was not one, and he could have got many more stones.

Lord Cockburn loved baths in a day when they were not too popular; and he constructed a basin in the bed of the Bonaly Burn, on its upper slopes, where he bathed in the early summer every day. It still is there.

The grounds are absolutely delightful; but after all, the greatest interest lies in the spirits which ought to haunt it, if they do not— Jeffrey, Brougham, Francis Horner, Sydney Smith, Professor Pillans, and a host of others of the great literary and legal people of Edinburgh's great past.

The Cockburns are an old Scottish family, and Henry was the fourth son of Archibald Cockburn of Cockpen. He was admitted a Member of the Faculty of Advocates of Edinburgh in 1800, became a Senator of the College of Justice in 1834, and died in 1854. He was one of the most popular men of his time in Edinburgh, a sound lawyer, and an excellent judge. His *Memorials* are interesting reading, although the book is not a model of good English. One of his stories makes the sardonic old judge, Lord Braxfield, live again as a humorist. " Almost the only story of him I ever heard," wrote Cockburn, " that had some fun in it without immodesty, was when a butler gave up his place because his lordship's wife was always scolding him. ' Lord,' he exclaimed, ' ye've little to complain o'; ye may be thankfu' ye're no mairrit to her.' " It is quite in line with his remark to an accused who had made an eloquent defence, " Ye're a vera clever chiel, man, but ye'll be nane the waur o' a guid hangin'."

X

BORTHWICK CASTLE, GOREBRIDGE, MIDLOTHIAN

THERE is a village of Borthwick, placed on the rising ground which forms the lower slopes of the Moorfoot Hills; and on a clear day, of which there are many in the neighbourhood, a beautiful view unfolds itself, including the whole country which lies between that point and Arthur's Seat. The greatest and most attractive feature of Borthwick is its castle, which is one of the finest of its type in the whole of Scotland. It is also notable as standing now in practically its original form, although it is known to have been built in the year 1430. It is not now surrounded by a demesne, but stands in the midst of fields. Its position is on the summit of a knoll anciently known as " the Mote of Locherwort." The river flows round it on the east and south, while the north side, on which there is now no water, is very steep and high; and this knoll may have had the water round its base in ancient days so as to form a moat.

On the west the castle is approached by level ground, but was there protected by a strong bastion tower in the corner of the surrounding wall. The castle itself has on that side a curious form, intended probably to increase its defensive properties. A broad and deep cleft in the side runs from foundation to parapet, making two wings, with extra windows in the opened space. But as the wings contain tiers of bedrooms, the device is not easily reconciled with pure defence. The handsome south-west bastion has been restored, and the entrance-gate of the courtyard stands beside it in the surrounding wall.

On entering the enclosed courtyard we pass round the south and east sides to arrive at the entrance in the north wall. The ground floor is occupied by vaulted cellars. The first floor, which contains the original baronial hall, is approached by the stair on the outside. This is the original position of the approach, which was by a " ramp " or " perron "—that is, a stair rising to a small platform about 14 feet from the doorway in the castle wall. A drawbridge lowered from the wall to the platform gave admittance to the friend. This ramp fell into ruins with the decay of the castle, but it has been well restored, and a stone landing carried on a half arch from the ramp to the wall takes the place of the drawbridge.

The length of the castle is 74 feet, the width 68 feet, and the height from base to battlement 90 feet. In the north-east corner of the first floor is a fine newel stair which has been restored from a condition of comparative ruin. At the foundations the thickness of the walls is 15 feet, but they get gradually thinner as they rise, until at the parapet they are only 6 feet thick. The parapet is supported on a triple line of fine corbelling, and there are the usual roof buildings.

The hall extends practically the whole length from north to south, with its present great window in the thickness of the wall, the form of the window being rectangular on the outside and arched inside in the Norman style, lighting a passage from east to west which is cut out of the dimensions of the hall.

This passage is reached by the newel stair, the great hall occupying two storeys. Above the window is another similarly shaped, but shorter, and beautifully arched on the inside. It lights the present drawing-room, which is a large hall very like that beneath it. Above this is another hall of great dimensions which was a barrack-room for the men-at-arms. On the south side of the present drawing-room floor a section of the whole width from east to west is cut off, one portion being the chapel, while another part, on the west side, is known as " Queen Mary's Room."

The entrance was not only protected by the ramp and bridge, but also by a guard-room in the thickness of the wall within the doorway. A stair which led from the basement to this landing came out beside the guard-room; so that it was impossible for access to be obtained to the living-rooms without the intruder being seen. The kitchen is on the right of this entrance, in one of the peculiar west wings, and has an immense fireplace.

On the east side the masonry on the level of the drawing-room and barrack-room is rough and much broken, the result of a cannonading which Cromwell gave it. And the wall is thinner than usual on that side because of the great fireplace of the drawing-room. On the south side of the surrounding wall is a ruined bastion, one of the four or six which formed the original defence.

A striking feature of the main hall is its great height. Its roof is beautifully arched, and the room has always been regarded as the finest and most elegantly proportioned of all such halls in Scotland. Nisbet described it thus : " It is so large and high in the roof that a man on horseback could turn a spear in it with all the ease imaginable." The stone roof was painted with devices like those in ancient illuminated manuscripts, and it is said that the inscription in Gothic lettering can still be made out—" Ye Temple of Honour."

BORTHWICK CASTLE
FROM THE SOUTH-WEST

BORTHWICK CASTLE
THE NORTH FRONT. QUEEN MARY'S POSTERN
STANDS OPEN IN WALL ON LEFT

But I failed to make it out on account of the height. It has two striking monuments of the olden time—a minstrel gallery and a fine old fireplace, the latter flanked by handsome columns.

The drawing-room above the main hall has a floor and ceiling of wood, the ceiling on beams which stretch from west to east. Its arched windows in the thickness of the walls give it marked character. The small room reached from it in the south-west corner is said to be that which Mary Queen of Scots used. All sorts of odd rooms, passages, and stairs are to be met in bewildering number. Restoration has added nothing to this ancient house, and has taken nothing away. Its ancient warrior owners would be at home in it if they could reappear.

A very curious incident is mentioned in the *New Statistical Account of Scotland* on the authority of Sir Walter Scott, who is stated to have published his authority in an extract from the Consistory Register of St. Andrews. It took place in the year 1547, when a macer of the Archidiocesan Court was sent to intimate the excommunication of Lord Borthwick. It was the time of the carnival of the " Abbot of Unreason," and the festive procession proceeded to duck the macer in the mill-pond. As the period of the Abbot's " misrule " was about Christmas, the ducking must have been unpleasant. The crowd next took the poor man, whose name was William Langlands, to the church to be fed. The food consisted of his own writ of parchment, torn into small pieces to make them more digestible, and conveyed in a bowl of wine. Then he was sent home. A full account is given in a note to " The Abbot."

The origin of the family of Borthwick is attributed to a Lord of Burtick in Livonia, but that is really legendary, although it receives colour from the further claim that the Borthwicks came to Scotland with Queen Margaret in 1067. Two Sir Williams of the name occupied the neighbouring Catcune, father and son; and a third Sir William, son of the second, built Borthwick Castle, having received a licence to do it from James III. In 1430 he was created Lord Borthwick. Recumbent effigies of him and his lady survive, and are in an old chapel attached to the new church and now used as a " session house."

Two historical incidents attest the loyalty of the Borthwicks to the Crown. On June 11, 1567, Queen Mary and the Earl of Bothwell, then her husband, were at Borthwick, when the barons, with a thousand men, thought to capture them. But Bothwell got warning and departed quickly, while Mary, " in mennes claithes, butit and spurrit, departit the samin night of Borthwick to Dunbar." Poor Mary ! She lost her way on the moor and at

last found shelter in Cakemuir Castle, where her room is still shown.
After that came Carberry, and she was soon a Queen without a
crown. The other incident was Cromwell's attack.

The title has passed through many vicissitudes, and is now
dormant; but the present owner, Henry Borthwick, is the *de jure*
baron, who has not claimed.

XI

BOTURICH CASTLE, LOCH LOMOND

BOTURICH CASTLE, which is the property of Major R. E. Findlay, is situated about five and a half miles due north of Dumbarton, and about two and a half miles from Balloch, in the county of Dumbarton. It lies along the curve of the shores of Loch Lomond on the south-east, where the loch narrows rapidly to form the River Leven, which carries the waters to the estuary of the Clyde. The present estate includes Knockour, Lorn, and Little Blairlinnans, and slopes from fairly high ground on the east down to the shores of the loch. The situation is exceedingly beautiful.

On the estate the residence is not an old house in the strict meaning of the words, as it was built later than 1830; but it incorporates what was left of the really ancient castle and historical stronghold, which had fallen into complete ruin by the year 1830. The old walls form the lower parts of the main block of the present building on the south and east sides, which exhibit the ancient features of a Scottish residential fortress; and thus continuity of history and sentiment is well maintained.

The old building had originally belonged to the Lennox family, and formed one of the chain of forts which were built to put a stop to the depredations of the Highlanders, who were in the habit of descending from their mountain fastnesses into the Lowlands, collecting all the valuables which they could find in a hasty raid, and driving home before them a goodly stock of Lowland cattle before an effective force could be raised to resist them.

The lands passed through many hands in the course of time. In 1830 the owner was John Buchanan of Ardoch, who had already built Balloch Castle, an old Balloch Castle having by that time completely disappeared, although its ancient fosse survived. Mr. Buchanan worked on the surviving walls of Boturich soon after 1830, and in 1850 added the "Octagon Tower," in which is the principal entrance. Mary, daughter of John Buchanan, had married Robert Findlay of Easterhill, and the builder sold the property to his son-in-law. Robert Findlay died without issue and left the property to his father, who in turn left it to his son, Colonel John

41

Findlay. Colonel Findlay sold it to his brother Charles, whose son, the present owner, inherited it. Four generations of the present family have accordingly held the estate, but in a very curious succession.

The avenue, which strikes off from a somewhat rough road, is very well wooded, and presents the first view of the castle as we round one of its curves—and that view shows a house which looks about 200 years older than it is, and in perfect harmony with its natural surroundings. From one of the heights on the north we see Inchmurrin lying on the bosom of the loch to the north-west, while to the north we see a multitude of islands dotting the expanse of water as far as the eye can reach.

In the " Octagon Tower " the entrance is surmounted by a coat of arms and the motto " Fortis in Arduis." The hall is adorned with the heads and antlers of stags, trophies of the neighbourhood. A handsome staircase leads to the first and principal floor, and is continued in the opposite direction. At the head of the first flight of steps is a large painting, occupying practically the whole wall, representing Colonel John Findlay standing by his horse. This was presented in 1875 by the Dumbartonshire Rifle Volunteers to Colonel Findlay, who had been the commanding officer many years.

To the right runs a passage eastward, leading to the drawing-room and dining-room, the latter of which contains a painting of the youthful Duke of Monmouth, which has come to the present owner through the family of de Cardonnel from the Duke's daughter Mary, who married James de Cardonnel. Their son, Mansfeldt Cardonnel, Commissioner of Customs at Musselburgh, appears in Smollett's *Humphrey Clinker* in the letter to Dr. Lewis signed " Matt. Bramble " and dated " Edinb., July 18th ": " At Musselburgh, however, I had the good fortune to drink tea with my old friend Mr. Cardonnel." The other rooms in the house are just such as one would expect to see, and one of them contains an interesting drawing of the old castle as it was in 1830.

When Sir Walter Scott was preparing his material for *Rob Roy* he visited the owner of the castle, the John Buchanan already mentioned, to see the double-handed sword which had belonged to the famous outlaw. But as the novel was published in 1829 Sir Walter's entertainment was at Balloch Castle, although it is more than likely that he visited the old ruin of Boturich.

The old house and the neighbourhood have associations of the most intense interest. At the end of the fifteenth century, when the

BOTURICH CASTLE
LOOKING NORTH-WEST
TO LOCH LOMOND

BOTURICH CASTLE
THE ENTRANCE PORCH

old Earldom of Lennox was broken up, Boturich came into the hands of the family of Haldane, in the person of John Haldane of Gleneagles. This knight was killed at Flodden in 1513, and his wife continued to live at Boturich, possibly as guardian of their son. But on an occasion when she was at Gleneagles Boturich was raided and captured by Macfarlane of Arrocher. The incident gave rise to a famous poem of Sir David Lindsay of the Mount, whose literary excellence is practically unknown to his countrymen, doubtless on account of the archaic spelling. But scholars appreciate him. He was born about the year 1490, was in his youth a personal attendant of Prince James who became James V., became Lyon Herald, and died about 1555.

The poem is entitled " The Historie of Squyer William Meldrum of Cleische and Bynnis." It runs to nearly 1,600 lines, and records the adventures of a doughty Scottish youth of good family, who was:

> " Ane Gentilman of Scotland borne,
> So was his father him beforne :
> Of nobilnes lineallie descendit,
> Quhilkis thair gude fame hes ever defendit."

This youth distinguished himself in arms wherever he went, and is described as saving a beautiful girl from two barbarous soldiers in an attack upon " Craigfergus " in a naval war with England, in which he appears to have been in the service of the King of France. When he returned to Scotland he was the darling of the ladies as the ideal knight. He had a kind of triumphal progress, but did not fall to the charms of any until in passing through Strathnairne " of ane castell he gat ane sicht " as the night was approaching. So he stopped there; and the poet says:

> " Of this triumphand plesand place,
> Ane lustie ladie wes maistres,
> Quhais lord wes deid schort tyme befoir,
> Quhairthrow hir dolour wes the moir:
> Bot yit scho tuke sum comforting,
> To heir the plesant dulce talking,
> Of this young squyer, of his chance,
> And how it fortunit him in France."

The two fell in love, and he tarried a long time, awaiting a dispensation to marry the lady. While thus engaged, the news arrived of Macfarlane's raid on Boturich, for the lady was none other than Dame Marjorie or Marion Haldane, a daughter of

43

Lawson of Humbie, Provost of Edinburgh. When Squire Meldrum heard the news:

> " In till his hart thair grew sic ire,
> That all his bodie brint in fyre;
> And sewoir it sud be full deir sald,
> Gif he micht him in that hald."

So he set out for Boturich, where he and " Macferland " put up a mighty fight, in which the Squire was victorious. He put a lieutenant in charge and returned to the arms of his " ladie." His history was not as happy as it ought to have been afterwards. While he and the lady were on their way to Edinburgh, not yet married, a rival ambushed and grievously wounded him. He survived, very much crippled, but the lady was forcibly married to someone else, and the Squire and she never saw each other again. The poem is not mere romance: it is history, and there are many details known which I have not recorded.

XII

BROOMHALL, DUNFERMLINE, FIFE

BROOMHALL is very near the northern shore of the Firth of Forth, with the town of Dunfermline a little more than two miles to the north-east. The present house is largely modern, and is built in the classical style, with its entrance front facing the north and its length from west to east. Its predecessor was built about the year 1650, and is incorporated in the north part of the frontage; but it is hardly possible now to separate any part from the rest and to describe it as belonging to the old house. The late Earl of Elgin remembered the north front in an unfinished state, the porch being then unbuilt, and its site represented by a gap between the two wings, with the old house showing through the gap.

The house contains three storeys, the lowest on the north front being slightly sunk, and the stonework of the rustic pattern. The south front is more striking than the north. The centre part corresponds with the porch of the north front, but its line curves outward, appealing to the eye rather as a segment of an ellipse than of a circle, and giving an impression of the Greek rather than the Roman classical idea. Six rounded columns support a continuous entablature above the windows, while under the entablature, and above each window, is a marble panel containing a classical figure. The south side receives the sunshine generously and has a wide expanse of garden, lawn, and park. The ends of the house are somewhat plain, and their similarity to each other continues the symmetrical design.

The entrance-hall on the north front is a magnificent room, with a floor of beautiful white marble which came from Greece. The mention of Greece at once brings up the memory of the famous Earl of Elgin, great-grandfather of the present earl. It was that earl who brought to England the famous marbles which are so great a treasure of the British Museum. And it was that earl who built the south front of Broomhall. Besides his famous collection of marbles in the British Museum, he made a smaller collection which is still in this house.

45

The hall contains part of this collection, and also a series of seven paintings which at one time had a place in the Luxembourg Palace. Two of them have a special interest for Scotland, namely, " The Marriage of James V. of Scotland with Magdalene, daughter of Francis I. of France," and " The Marriage, by Proxy, of James V. of Scotland with Mary of Lorraine." The former of these ceremonies was one of great magnificence, but the poor bride died after about six months in Scotland. Tytler's *History of Scotland* describes the ceremony in the following words: " The marriage was celebrated in the Church of Notre Dame with the utmost pomp and magnificence. The kings of France and Navarre and many illustrious foreigners surrounded the Altar, and the Church lent a peculiar solemnity to the ceremony by the presence of seven cardinals." Mary Queen of Scots, was the child of the second marriage.

However great is the interest of these famous paintings, it is excelled by that of the Greek marbles. A very interesting description of the whole collection at Broomhall was published in *The Journal of Hellenic Studies* in 1884 by Ad. Michaelis; and, so far as I am aware, that is the only detailed description which exists. They are mostly in Pentelic marble, the same kind of stone of which the Parthenon is built; and they are mostly *stelæ*, or, to put it in English, tombstones. Many of them are built into the walls, and some of them have inscriptions. One of these contains three figures in high relief, whose names were Theogenis, Nikodemos, and Nikomache. It is a beautiful piece of work, which might easily stimulate the imagination to create a story which should explain why these three people were associated on one tombstone.

An old stone chair stands in the hall—a marble throne with reliefs on the back. It is described in Stakelberg's *Graber der Hellenen*, and was seen by that writer about the year 1810 on the site of the ancient Prytaneion, or town hall. In 1835 he was still under the impression that it was on the ancient site, but another writer had in 1811 noted its transfer to the Earl of Elgin. In the meantime it was lost to knowledge in England, and only reappeared when Michaelis noted its presence at Broomhall.

One group in the reliefs is believed by Michaelis to represent Theseus slaying the Amazon, while another represents Harmodios and Aristogeiton slaying the despot Hipparchos in 514 B.C.

Close to the chair a sepulchral *stele* of Myttion in the wall has an interest of a special kind, throwing light on the ancient treatment of sculptures. Along the two sloping edges faint traces of a painted *hymation*, or robe, are visible. An inscription is clear on the horizontal stripe just above the field of relief, and that

BROOMHALL
THE NORTH FRONT

BROOMHALL
THE WEST END

inscription was never cut by hand. It had been painted. And the paint preserved the stone under it while the weather cut the stone around it for 2,300 years. The *stele* is remarkable for its excellent preservation, and suggests that many stones which now have no inscriptions had them in paint at one time. Another remarkable fact is that it bears in flat relief the figure of a girl with short curling hair, in the pose of walking, and wearing a very uncommon dress— a long, ungirdled *chiton*, with a stiff plain jacket over it descending to the knees. The jacket has long sleeves, and is exactly that worn by Albanian women in the present day.

One of the marbles shows the religion of the departed. Two females stand facing us, that on the left being shorter and more thickset than the other. She wears a *chiton* and *chlamys*, and her hair is carefully arranged in parallel lines. The taller is a priestess of Isis, wearing a *chiton* and fringed mantle, and holding in her uplifted hand a *seistron*, a metallic rattle used in the rites of Isis. There are two inscriptions, one on the left carefully done and one on the right barbaric. They are—*Aphrodisia Olympou Salameinia* and *Patanaiath Quosanea*. The only thing revealed with certainty is that the *stele* is in memory of Aphrodisia of the island of Salamis, and that she adopted the religion of the Egyptian Isis. There are many other marbles, one being a complete sarcophagus, with an inscription which identifies the burial as that of Ailios Epikrates Berenikides, son of Ailios Zeno, who was an " interpreter of religious rites " between 197 and 207 B.C.

Passing directly through the hall we enter the library. From it is entered the drawing-room. The dining-room is to the north of the drawing-room; and the library, a large and handsome room where all the rooms are admirable, is lighted by the three windows of the south front. The dining-room contains a chimney-piece made out of a grand old bed, finely carved, which was originally in the Palace of Dunfermline and belonged to Anne of Denmark, wife of James VI. of Scotland and I. of England, and the mother of Charles I., who was born at Dunfermline.

The family name of the Earl of Elgin is Bruce; and the Elgin branch descends from the same stem as King Robert Bruce, through the Bruces of Clackmannan. There is no certain evidence of the point at which the Bruces of Clackmannan left the stem, but the old and undisputed tradition is that they are descended from John, a younger son of Robert de Brus, 5th Lord of Annandale. It is known from English records that Robert had a fourth son of that name. Thomas de Brus is the first proved owner of Clackmannan, and he died before 1348. The sword and helmet of King Robert Bruce are at Broomhall, left to the Earl at the end of the eighteenth century by Katherine Bruce, widow of Henry, the last of the Bruces of Clackmannan who held lands.

The present laird is the 10th Earl of Elgin and the 14th Earl of Kincardine. The Earl of the Marbles was Thomas, the 7th and 11th. Byron was very unjust to him about them, in *Childe Harold, The Curse of Minerva,* and *English Bards and Scotch Reviewers.* The late earl had a most distinguished career. He received the honour of a Knighthood of the Garter, and held the great office of Viceroy of India, after having shown his ability in other administrative offices.

Besides the antiquities which have already been mentioned, there is a very fine collection of Greek vases, chiefly Lekithoi from Athens, some of them belonging to a very early date.

XIII

CALLENDAR HOUSE, FALKIRK

IN many respects Callendar House, the residence of Charles William Forbes of Callendar, is one of the most interesting and remarkable houses in Scotland. In itself, it is a very fine and impressive structure on account of its size and its architecture. It contains a great many articles of personal and historical association, and its rooms have been occupied by people whose names live in the history and romance of our country. It is a house which has grown, and it is doubtful whether the most learned of architectural antiquaries could say with certainty into how many periods the house should be divided. There are parts of the walls 8½ feet thick. And there is a piece of wall which is said to be of Roman workmanship. On the interior this part was lined with painted oak panels, which were removed about twelve years ago to be cleared of the paint and replaced, and it was then that the character of the masonry was discovered.

Speculation in this case is helped by positive history and antiquarian research, for not far from the north front, and roughly parallel with it, runs through the park a section of Antonine's Wall, the great wall built in A.D. 142 by Lollius Urbicus, under orders from the Emperor Antoninus Pius, to keep off the northern tribes. Along the wall ran a great military road, with stone forts at intervals, largely following the line of Agricola's Wall, built in A.D. 80. Between these dates and the withdrawal of the Romans about the year 410 there was ample time for the building of stone houses as well as forts. There is some reason, therefore, for the belief that there has been a house on the site since the time of the Romans.

From the west lodge there is an avenue which sweeps past the house to the east lodge, approaching and leaving the house by curves, and very charmingly wooded. The entrance front faces the north, and the ground gives the impression that the house is built on a natural knoll. On a rough measurement the whole line of the house is not less than 300 feet. It also has height and mass. There is a wing on each side lower than the central mass, which projects in front of the line of the wings. The old house of the historic days had a courtyard where the central part faced by the porch now stands. That part has been built since 1818, when Alexander Nasmyth made a drawing of the building. The general aspect of the whole edifice as seen on the north side is one of towers, turrets, parapets, crow-stepped end gables, stone chimneys, beautiful windows, conical roofs to towers and turrets, stone visible on the centre front, and the wings and extensions " harled "—that is, plastered roughcast. It shows a very charming whole.

The south front shows a very symmetrical design on a long line. The centre part adheres to the general line of the old house. In front on this side is an extensive terrace a few feet higher than the park above which it stands, guarded by a low parapet wall, the centre of which is broken to allow of steps down to the lower level. Many of the rooms on the ground floor have the original vaulted stone roofs. It is in the eastern part of the south front, between a balcony and a round tower, that the supposed Roman wall exists; and it forms an interior wall of the staircase which is known as the " King Charles I. Staircase." But this name is only used to indicate the period to which it belongs, and it is not claimed that King Charles I. ever used it.

A lovely view of this front is obtained from a small loch which lies a short distance eastward. Further east there is a remarkable mausoleum in the Greek style, built by the first William Forbes, who bought the Callendar estate in 1783. It is believed to be a copy of a Greek temple, but bears a certain resemblance, with differences, to the " Ædes Vestæ " of Rome, now known as the church of S. Stefano delle Carozze. It contains a Greek inscription, perhaps by Lucian, the Christian satirist of the second century, and has been put into English verse in these words:

> " All things we mortals call our own
> Are mortal too and quickly flown;
> But could they all for ever stay,
> We soon from them must pass away."

The tradition which claims a house here ever since Roman times says that it and the lands were held on the tenure of supplying the army of occupation with billets of wood for their military works, a service believed to have been continued into later days. Then there is the very confused legend of the Graham who is said to have given his name to the Roman Wall as Grime's Dyke, and who was buried in the old church of Falkirk, according to an inscribed slab which was found when the church was demolished in 1810. At a short distance from the south front is an old sundial, bearing a

CALLENDAR HOUSE
THE NORTH FRONT

CALLENDAR HOUSE
THE SOUTH FRONT

coronet and the coat of arms of the family of the Earls of Kilmarnock, so dating from about the year 1722.

A long leap back in the centuries takes us to the year 1345, when Sir William Livingston received a grant of the barony of Callendar, forfeited by Sir Patrick de Callendar, and strengthened his right by marrying the only child and heiress.

It was through another forfeiture that William Forbes became the owner. The 5th Earl of Linlithgow and 4th Earl of Callendar was attainted and his estates forfeited for his part in " the 'fifteen." In 1720 the York Buildings Company bought the estate and leased it to the Earl of Kilmarnock, who had married a daughter of the Earl of Callendar. They were tenants in 1745, and Lord Kilmarnock was executed for his part in the attempt of that year. Lady Kilmarnock's son succeeded to the title of Earl of Errol, and the family always wanted to get the estate back. So, when it was put up for sale in 1783 owing to the difficulties of the York Buildings Company, there was a general abstention from offers in order that the family should get it at a low price.

To the consternation of those present, William Forbes made an offer of the " upset " price, and there was no representative of the Errol family present to bid against him. Report says that someone whispered to the auctioneer to demand " payment in cash " on the spot; but William Forbes was ready, and presented a currency note, of some kind of legal tender, for £100,000, and demanded " change." So he won.

He had made his money by supplying the Admiralty with copper for bottoming ships—when it was a new idea—and he had "cornered" the market in readiness for the deal. Then he bought it back cheaply on account of a temporary failure of the method, and sold it again to the Admiralty when the invention was perfected. At least, that is the story; and it gives rise to another.

He had a difference with a parish minister about the rent of a field, invited the minister to dinner, and got it arranged. But the minister repented of his bargain made over the dinner or the bottle. And the following Sunday he preached from the text, 2 Tim. iv. 14: " Alexander the coppersmith did me much evil; the Lord reward him according to his works."

The interior is almost finer than the exterior. The hall is finely panelled in old oak, with a main staircase in two flights, and a landing which forms a gallery above. The dining-room is of magnificent proportions—about 100 feet long and 30 wide. The gallery has several pieces of charming Spanish pictorial tapestry. A magnificent Raeburn is in the morning-room—a full-length of

William Forbes. The drawing-room has a great collection of mirrors, some of them dating from the time of the attainted Earl.

Of all the rooms in the house, sentiment and interest turn to a few which are associated with Mary Queen of Scots, and we can almost sense her presence. Two of them open into each other, and above the communicating doorway is an inscription: " Queen Mary of Scots and her ladies occupied these rooms and those above them, August 12, 1562; July 1, 1565; January 13, 1567; January 24, 1567; and January 29, 1567."

XIV

CAPRINGTON CASTLE, KILMARNOCK

CAPRINGTON CASTLE lies about two miles to the south-west of Kilmarnock, in the parish of Riccarton, and is the property of Major W. Wallace Cuninghame, who not long ago succeeded his father, the late Lieutenant-Colonel John A. S. Cuninghame, of Caprington, Ayrshire, and Auchlochan, Lanarkshire. A first view of the building gives the impression of a great mansion, merely modern. But not only does it occupy the site of an ancient stronghold—it also embodies a great deal of the old fortress. Up till 1820 the old castle remained in practically its original condition, additions having merely been tacked on from time to time, some of them simply of the nature of outhouses. The late Colonel Cuninghame completed the building as it is now, but its design dates from the year 1797, in the time of Sir William Cuninghame, 4th Baronet of Lambrughton, who gave it all its present essential features in 1820.

A very attractive avenue, well wooded, leads on a slight ascent from the Kilmarnock road. The four fronts of the house face the cardinal points, with the main entrance in the east front. The Todrigs Burn flows through the policies and encloses the castle in a kind of loop, leaving the south side clear, and flowing almost parallel with the River Irvine about three-quarters of a mile before joining it. The site is rising ground, with a flat-topped rock protruding to a height of about 10 feet above the summit, and originally about 50 feet long, with something approaching that in width. This allowed room for the building of a " keep " 48 feet long and 33 broad, with sufficient surface left free for a stair and approach. All this indicates a remote date for the old castle.

The old natural rock, at one time visible, is now concealed by the new masonry of the south-east part of the block. On the sides which fall away from the angle it is as if the rock had been buttressed by continuous masonry, sloping inwards as it rises. At a height which is presumably that of the old rock a terrace runs along the sides and has a plain parapet. At each of the angles of the two fronts is a round bastion, the three towers giving a great sense of

53

massiveness and strength, although they do not rise above the height of the wall. The terrace occupies the whole of the ground floor level, broken on the east front by the great porch; and this ground floor is occupied by vaulted rooms or cellars.

The porch projects 24 feet in front of the terrace wall, and has three wide and flattened Gothic arches, each outer angle of the porch supported by a massive round buttress turret. Above the front arch is the coat of arms on a projecting part of the parapet. The general aspect of the east front presents a great central octagon tower with three of its faces to the front, while the angles have slender square buttress towers.

On the south front there is a greater appearance of age. At its west end is a turn to the north, carrying us to a lower terrace with a door into the dining-room. The lower storeys in this part are old; and the drawing-room seems to correspond with the " keep." The original stair of that building is still there, and served the new buildings which were added towards the end of the sixteenth century.

The interior of the house is as attractive as the exterior. From the great porch, with its groined roof, a flight of fifteen steps rises to the first floor, which is in many respects the real ground floor of the house, as it is the platform made by the summit of the rock. Here is the hall, above which rises a great open space or " well," lighted from the roof. On the west side is the main staircase. On the drawing-room landing, which has an oak ceiling over the fore-part, are three figures in full plate armour, interesting in themselves as showing the fighting equipment of a knight of old.

The drawing-room is directly to the south of the " well," and has a very handsome ceiling carried on beams which cross the room and which maintain the Gothic scheme of architecture and orna-mentation which pervades the castle. There are some excellent paintings, one of special interest being that of Sir William Dick, of Prestonfield, born in 1761, to whose family went the Cuninghame baronetcy as well as that of Dick.

The dining-room is in line with the drawing-room on the south side, and is in an old part of the house, though perhaps not in the oldest part. It used to form the kitchen and pantry, and it was transformed by the late Colonel Cuninghame. On the north wall it has a painting of his father and his father's two sisters.

The present Laird was a Captain in the 2nd Life Guards when the Great War began, and was wounded in the first Battle of Ypres, returning to the Front in 1915. In 1918 he was acting Lieutenant-Colonel commanding the 9th Cheshires, and received the D.S.O.

CAPRINGTON CASTLE
THE EAST FRONT

CAPRINGTON CASTLE
THE DINING ROOM

for his leading of a brilliant counter-attack in which his horse was shot under him. He gained his objective without hurt, but was severely wounded while handing over the position to a relieving battalion.

There is an agelong inheritance of national service on the part of the Laird of Caprington, from the uncle of Sir William Wallace to the present time. The uncle of Sir William Wallace was Sir Richard Wallace, and he lived at Caprington. But a previous Sir Richard Wallace was " of Riccarton," the parish in which Caprington is situated, and is believed to have received the lands from Walter, the High Steward, who died about the year 1177. The name is probably a form of Walays or Valence, and doubtless the knight Sir Aymer de Valence of Sir Walter Scott's *Castle Dangerous* bore a variant of the name. In the Latin *Protocolla* quoted in the *Diocesan Registers of Glasgow*, the name is frequently mentioned in association with the lands of Ellerslie and Craigie, the spelling of the names being " Walles," " Cragy," and " Ellirsly." It is interesting to note that Sir William Wallace, the only real and disinterested patriot of his day among the leaders, was most probably of Norman blood, like those whom he opposed.

The list of Lairds would show an uninterrupted blood succession from those distant days, twice passing through the female line, and not even broken by one instance of transfer by purchase, for the sale was made to a cousin of the same family and name with no child to succeed. A lady of the Wallace family carried the estate into the Cuninghame family in the fourteenth century; and in the nineteenth century a lady of that family inherited, her husband taking the name of Cuninghame, which still remains.

The first Cuninghame of Caprington was a grandson of Sir William Cuninghame of Kilmaurs, who married Elinor, granddaughter of Edward Bruce, and became in her right Earl of Carrick. Sir William's eldest son was ancestor of the Earls of Glencairn; and a son of his second son was William Cuninghame, who married the daughter of Sir Richard Wallace of Caprington, uncle of the patriot, and received Caprington as her marriage portion. The date of this marriage is given as 1325.

The next lady who took Caprington with her was Anne, daughter of the fourth baronet of the family of Dick of Prestonfield. The inheritance of the Dick baronetcy went through Janet, only surviving child of Sir James Dick of Prestonfield, who had married Sir William Cuninghame, Baronet, of Caprington—but with the condition that the name of Cuninghame was to be dropped in favour of that of Dick. So Lady Cuninghame's eldest son became Sir John Cuninghame, while her second and third sons became in turn Sir William and Sir Alexander Dick. Anne Dick was a daughter of Sir Alexander Dick—a Dick by name and a Cuninghame by blood. She ultimately became the owner of Caprington and the senior representative of the family of Cuninghame of Caprington. And she married John Smith, who took her name. The present Laird is their great-grandson.

XV

CARBERRY TOWER, MUSSELBURGH, MIDLOTHIAN

NOT far from the historic Roman station at Inveresk is Carberry Tower, the residence of Lord Elphinstone, K.T., a representative of an old Scottish family which has given many eminent members to the service of Church and State. And in the grounds of Carberry Tower is the historic Carberry Hill, the meeting on which meant the loss of the Crown to Mary Queen of Scots. If we pursue further the road by which we reach Carberry, following the rising ground, and then descending to the left, we come to Elphinstone Tower, the original home and stronghold of the Elphinstone family.

Carberry Tower is vastly different now from what it was in ancient days. It is situated in an extensive park, beautifully wooded, and with attractive gardens. The principal avenue runs direct from the public road to the Tower. The entrance front, which faces west, consists of an original oblong block, built for strength, to which the other parts of the residence have been added from time to time. The front is to a large extent covered with climbing plants, which give it a very charming appearance.

The main entrance is to the left of the old tower, and admits to a spacious hall which might be described as two halls joined by a passage. From the inner of the two divisions rises a wide stair, on mounting which we come to the drawing-room and the libraries. An attractive feature of the drawing-room is that at each end of the front wall there is a small room adorned with miniatures and other portraits. There are two libraries, one north and one south. In the north room are two busts, one of them of the 13th Lord Elphinstone, and the other of his uncle, the Honourable Mountstuart Elphinstone, fourth son of the eleventh baron, and famous for his career in India. He entered the service of the East India Company in 1795, took part in Wellesley's campaign in 1803, and was appointed Commissioner at Berar in 1804. In 1807 he was sent as the first British envoy to Cabul, which must have required a vast amount of steady courage. His acquaintance with the languages and character of the inhabitants of India, together with all that he did for Indian education during his various appointments, made him in his day the first authority on Indian affairs. From 1819 to 1827 Mountstuart Elphinstone was Governor of Bombay.

The south library contains a collection of illuminated Oriental manuscripts and books which must be of great literary value.

The dining-room contains two specially interesting paintings. One is of the famous Bishop William Elphinstone, who lived from 1431 till 1514. He was Rector of Glasgow University, Archdeacon of Argyll, and Bishop of Ross, before he became Bishop of Aberdeen and Lord High Chancellor of Scotland. He founded Aberdeen University.

The other is that which the artist—or some other person—inscribed " James VIII., King of Scotland," and which also carries the inscription: " Peint par A. S. Belle, 1717." There is a whole pathetic story in the picture and the inscriptions; and the picture is a very interesting painting.

Another interesting room is the armoury, although it is small as a room. It is filled with a great variety of the implements of war, some belonging to the ancient days of our own country, and others examples of the weapons of the uncivilised races of the modern world. The late Lord Elphinstone, father of the present Baron, had been a Captain in the Royal Navy, and took a great interest in forming the collection. In later years many friends added to the collection as they returned from various parts of the world.

Something less than twenty years ago the present Lord Elphinstone made a very great change in the south front of the house. The west end of that front remains practically unaltered. The east end had as its principal feature a large bay window thrown out from the wall on tiers of corbelling, and had above it a battlemented parapet similar to that which crowned the whole wall. For this was substituted a tall slender projecting bay, which rose one storey higher and has a crow-stepped gable. The slim bartizans of that part have disappeared. The centre part of the face was remodelled, a very good window on the first floor remaining unchanged. The battlemented parapet has gone, its place being taken by a crow-stepped gable, while short and broad round bartizans rise from the level of the top of the centre window. Dormer windows were placed in the roof, which was raised and received a greater slope. The full effect of the alterations is extremely pleasing, and in complete keeping with the general style of the house, following generally the lines which already were those of the east front.

Carberry Hill has on it a monolith with the inscription: " At this spot Mary Queen of Scots, after the escape of Bothwell, mounted her horse and surrendered herself to the Confederate lords,

CARBERRY TOWER
THE SOUTH FRONT

CARBERRY TOWER
PART OF THE SUNK GARDEN

June 15, 1567." Not far away is another stone, with this inscription: " These entrenchments were thrown up by the English before the battle of Pinkie, September 10, 1547, and afterwards made use of by Queen Mary, June 15, 1567." Here is compressed history.

Carberry Tower has only been in the Elphinstone family since 1802, and was reconstructed about 1830. But Carberry as a locality goes far back in the centuries. The lands were Crown property in the time of Malcolm Canmore, when there was a distinction between Inveresk Major and Inveresk Minor, both of which in time were gifted to the Abbey of Dunfermline. Towards the end of the fourteenth century the Abbey seems only to have retained the feudal superiority.

Little is known of Carberry, although it is the parish of the two Inveresks, until 1541, when Hugh Rigg, an Edinburgh Advocate, had a nineteen years' lease of the property. In 1543 George, Commendator of Dunfermline, gave Rigg a charter in feu farm. There is no mention of a residence before Hugh Rigg's time, which leads to a supposition that he built the tower, although it is quite likely that John de Crebarrie, a tenant of part of the Abbey lands at the end of the thirteenth century, had a dwelling of some kind. " Crebarrie " is an old form of the name Carberry, and the local pronunciation of " Carberry " throws the accent on the middle syllable.

Hugh Rigg either built or enlarged the tower, as proved by the extant couplet :

> " Auld Hugh Rigg was very big, but a bigger man was he
> When his cherubs chirpèd on his new tour of Carbere."

The " cherubs " were ornaments which he had placed on his mansion instead of the usual armorial symbols. Hugh Rigg built his place strongly, the tower being vaulted over the ground floor and under the roof, and the walls being 7 feet thick. He was a man of influence, to whom Calderwood, in his *History of the Kirk of Scotland*, practically attributes the defeat at Pinkie.

The Rigg family retained the Tower until 1659. In 1587 the church lands were annexed to the Crown, and King James gave the superiority of Carberry to Maitland of Thirlestane. It remained with that family—the Lauderdale family—until Anne, Duchess of Monmouth and Buccleuch, purchased it. The Rigg family was succeeded by Sir Adam Blair, who was deprived at the Revolution of 1689; and he was followed by Sir Robert Dickson of Inveresk, who sold Carberry to John Fullerton, designated " of Carberry."

From him the estate descended to his niece, Elizabeth Fullerton, eldest daughter of William Fullerton of Carstairs. She married the Honourable William Elphinstone, third son of the 10th Baron Elphinstone, and her husband added her name to his. Their son ultimately succeeded to the title, and thus came Carberry to the present family.

The old and original Elphinstone Tower is no ruin; it is a great block 50 feet long, 35 feet broad, and 58 feet high, with walls at the base 12 feet thick. Its owner, Sir Alexander Elphinstone, was killed in 1435 in the raid of Piperdean; and his daughter and heiress having married a Johnstone the Tower went with her, but after much litigation. It only returned by purchase a comparatively few years ago.

XVI

CASSILLIS HOUSE, MAYBOLE, AYRSHIRE

CASSILLIS HOUSE has been a centre of song and story, and
is bound up with the fortunes of the family of Kennedy, whose
influence in Scotland has been great. The name is derived
from the Gaelic *caiseal*, a fort, and is the same as " cashel " in Ireland,
where another race of Kennedys ruled. The parish of Kirkmichael,
in which the house stands, is diversified by wood and hill, by loch
and stream, and presents the appearance of a well-farmed and
comfortable countryside. Dunree and the Dounans are hillocks
in the old language, not far from the house, Dunree being in Gaelic
dun-righ, the hill-fort of the king, who is said by tradition to have
been the British King Coel or Coilus, King of Kyle—the " old King
Cole " who was a merry old soul. The Dounans are five little hills
opposite Cassillis House, and they were, and doubtless still are, the
abode of the fairies. They were celebrated by Burns in his poem
of " Halloween ":

> " Upon that night, when fairies light
> On Cassillis Downans dance,
> Or owre the lays, in splendid blaze,
> On sprightly coursers prance."

Tradition says that it was at first intended that Cassillis House or
Tower should occupy the summit of the highest of the Dounans.
Each night the fairies, who do most of their work at night, removed
the stones to another place, the present site ; and in time the humans
took the hint. The result is Cassillis House, of which the age is
unknown. Fairies often interfered in building operations in quite
a kindly way, as in the case of St. Oran's Chapel in Iona, and the
old chapel of Pennygown in Mull.

The oldest part of the house, a " peel " tower or " keep," is
built upon an outcrop of rock. The present frontage faces practically east, and the tower is on the south or south-west, to the left of
the visitor who is facing the entrance front. At the base is a walled
court, from which the walls rise straight until the summit is almost
reached, and at this point a continuous corbelling runs round the
building in four courses. At the corners are bartizans resting on the

general corbelling. Between the bartizans runs a handsome open balustrade of comparatively modern date, with a crow-stepped gable rising behind it.

The basement is vaulted, the walls graduated in thickness as they rise, from more than 16 feet on the ground and first floors to about 10 feet on the third floor. There is not a wall in the old house which has a uniform thickness throughout its length. Originally it had the customary great baronial hall, but that is now divided into two rooms. The *Statistical Account of Scotland* says that when this part was cleared in the earlier half of the last century a large quantity of human bones was removed. In 1789 a writer described the Tower as probably having undergone many repairs, but suggested that the appearance of the walls indicated the last repair as belonging to the time of Queen Mary or her son King James. The crow-stepped gable belongs to that period. In 1830 " an elegant Gothic addition," as it was then described, was made by the occupant, Lord Kennedy.

One very remarkable feature of the interior is found in connection with the stair which rises from the inner hall behind the outer entrance. The stair has four landings, and is an old part of the house. It is circular, and winds round a circular hollow column which until recently was covered with plaster. The tenant, Mr. John Strain, a well-known engineer, discovered that the column had contained windows. With the consent of the Marquis of Ailsa, who is the owner, he had the plaster removed, and laid bare a very handsome cylinder of stone, circular on the inside also. Windows appear at regular intervals, and on the inside there are stones projecting so as to appear to form steps from the bottom of the interior to the top. Some think that the immediate purpose was that of heating and lighting: now, at any rate, it is used for lighting, as electric lamps shine through the windows to light the stair.

In such an old house one expects to find curious rooms. Here one used to have the name of the " coffin room," entirely on account of its shape, without any superstition attached to it. The disagreeable name is now a mere memory, as the room has been divided into two. The same tenant who revealed the staircase windows made a further discovery in 1917. He decided to place a wooden dado round a small ancient room known as the "Aumrie," now a dressing-room. In plugging the wall the workman's tool went through into space, with the result that a " secret stair " was discovered—doubtless a strategic entrance and exit in ancient days.

The drawing-room is an attractive room with a handsome moulded plaster ceiling. An upper room looks down upon the

CASSILLIS HOUSE
FROM THE SOUTH-EAST

CASSILLIS HOUSE
"THE GIPSIES' STEPS" ON THE
RIVER DOON WITHIN THE GROUNDS

old courtyard, and is associated with an oft-told tale. The legend is that sometimes called " The Gipsy Countess," and is to be found in the old ballad of " Johnny Faa " in Pinkerton's *Select Scottish Ballads*, published in London in 1783. The outline of the legend may be grasped from the following stanzas:

> " The gipsies cam' to our gude lord's yett,
>   And O but they sang sweetly,
>   They sang sae sweet and sae vera complete
>   That doon cam' our fair ladie.

> " And she cam' tripping doun the stair,
>   And a' her maids before her ;
>   As soon as they saw her weel-faured face
>   They cuist the glamour o'er her.

> " Gae tak' frae me this gay mantile,
>   And bring tae me a plaidie ;
>   For though kith and kin and a' had sworn,
>   I'll follow the gipsy laddie."

So the lady and the gipsy leader, followed by his fifteen men, set off from the castle, but were soon pursued by the lord and overtaken after they had crossed the River Doon at the " Gipsies' Steps." The ballad gives the result in what purport to be the words of the only gipsy who survived the fight :

> " And we were fifteen well-made men,
>   Although we werena bonnie ;
>   And we were a' put down but ane,
>   For a fair young wanton ladie."

According to the legend, the leader was captured, and hanged next morning on the " Dule Tree " which still stands beside the house, the lady being compelled to witness the deed from her window.

In the ballad no names of place or person are mentioned, and it is entirely an oral legend which associates the incidents with Cassillis House and a Lord and Lady Cassillis : it cannot be too strongly emphasised that there is no foundation in the history of the family for any such association. And it is especially noted that the individual Lord and Lady Cassillis who are mentioned in the oral prose form of the tale are known to have lived happily.

It is a quaint and romantic legend, which seems to belong to any part of Europe, possibly carried from Eastern Europe by the gipsies when they arrived in Scotland. They were received hospitably at first as professedly persecuted Christian refugees from the East; but the country soon tired of them and was ready to hang them—as no doubt happened to many of them.

The same legend under a slightly different form appears in Robert Browning's poem " The Flight of the Duchess "—more diffuse, more artificial, more hazy to the comprehension, and with an atmosphere which retains its mid-European or Eastern suggestion.

XVII

COLSTOUN, HADDINGTON, EAST LOTHIAN

IN the east country of East Lothian there is a long road which runs from Dalkeith right into the Lammermuir Hills, by way of Ormiston, East Saltoun, and Gifford — old-world villages. And there is a road from Drem by the town of Haddington which runs into that road almost at right angles. On this road, about two miles from Haddington, is the mansion of Colstoun, in well-wooded grounds and in the midst of a delightful country rising gradually into the Lammermuirs to the south. Near the house is the Colstoun Water, which is just another name for the same stream which on another estate is called the Gifford Water.

Colstoun is a long house facing east and west, and " harled " on great part of its exterior, if not on all. The east face contains the entrance; and both fronts show a considerable variety of architecture due to the circumstance that the house may be said to have grown. On the west, for example, we see a round tower, typically Scottish, on its own foundation, and with a conical roof. But it only dates from 1860. Further to the right of the line is an octagon bay with five exterior faces topped by a parapet. Then comes a four-storeyed block with a bartizan turret at the north-west corner of the fourth storey, on three tiers of corbels. It almost escapes notice, and yet it tells part of the story of the building, for it was there before the fourth storey, and marks a boundary of the old house, suggesting a battlemented parapet which does not now exist.

Not far from the bartizan, and at about the same level, is a triangular slab in the wall, bearing the initials " P. B., E. R." which stand for Patrick Broun and Elizabeth Ramsay, who lived at Colstoun in the seventeenth century and may have added the storey. That gives the sixteenth century for the lower part and the bartizan. The estate of Colstoun, or Cumbercolstoun as it was named in the earliest charters, was a possession of the Broun family in the thirteenth century—how much earlier documents do not tell—and it is reasonable to think that they had a house there. There can be little doubt that the central block which has the little turret, now so inconspicuous, was that house or grew from it. A fire in 1907 made it necessary to rebuild a good deal of the block, and the walls were found to rest on foundations of the rudest description. A narrow staircase, which apparently led from the lowest room to the turret, was brought to light, and the joists of the room immediately above the chamber were found to be roughly shaped logs.

It seems probable that the original house was a small square tower with very thick walls. The south wing was added in 1903 by extending the line and raising by two storeys a low wing of uncertain age. The west front is high above the river. There is only a narrow path between the house and the sloping bank, with a walk at the bottom. On one occasion, in the highly convivial days when the legal lights of Edinburgh dined well into next morning, Charles Broun, an advocate and son of the Judge, Lord Colstoun, entertained some of them at Colstoun. One of them mistook the dining-room window for the door into the drawing-room, and rolled down the bank. He expostulated with his host in the words, " 'Od, Charlie Broun, what gars ye hae sic lang steps to your front door." The incident has been preserved by Dean Ramsay in his *Reminiscences of Scottish Life and Character*, as it was related to him by " Charlie " Broun's daughter, the Countess of Dalhousie.

The garden is divided into four parts by grass paths, with herbaceous borders and trellises covered with roses at the back of the borders. Where the grass walks intersect stands a sundial, and not far from it another sundial, with the date 1704, which long lay neglected in a corner but is now mounted on a modern pillar. There is a row of fine old sycamores, and a conspicuous object is an ancient round pigeon-house. In former days no Scottish house was complete without its dove-cot; and an old description of a typical Fife laird's possessions ran: " A wee pickle land, a gude pickle debt, and a doocot.

The main entrance is by a wide porch in the east front, which leads to a square entrance hall. A flight of steps, with a row of elephants' tusks on either side, carries us to the first floor, in which is a long corridor extending from the north end of the house to the smoking-room at the south end. It is the chief feature of the interior, and I do not know of anything quite like it in any other Scottish house. The ceiling is only 9 feet high, and the corridor was made by throwing four small rooms into the former centre passage, making wide recesses, each about 20 feet square. At the same time the gable end of the old block was pierced to give access to the new north wing. The ceilings of the modern part are 18 feet high—a great contrast to those of the old house. Among the interesting objects which fill the recesses are Sikh arms, Sikh flags, miniatures, china, tapestry and other works of art.

COLSTOUN
THE WEST FRONT

COLSTOUN
A CORNER OF THE GROUNDS
SHOWING THE " COLSTOUN WATER "

COLSTOUN, EAST LOTHIAN

A curious and treacherous weapon is shown—the wagnuck or tiger's claw, which often appears now in the pages of the kind of cheap novel known as a " blood." It can be hidden in the hollow of the hand, and has five sharp claws of steel. The holder pretends friendship, embraces his victim, and drives the claws into his back. Sivajee, who established the Mahratta power against the Mogul Emperor in the seventeenth century, is recorded to have used such a weapon. Tapestry worked by Lady Dalhousie; Oriental china and cases of Indian models of famous buildings such as the Taj Mahal ; portraits of Ranjit Singh and many Sikh Sirdars who fought against us in the Punjab—all these are to be seen in the recesses of the corridor. Those relating to India show the connection of the Dalhousie family with that Empire. The connection of the Broun family lies in this, that Christian, daughter of the Charles Broun of Dean Ramsay's story, and his heiress, married the 9th Earl of Dalhousie. It was she who told the Dean the story; and her son, the Marquis, had a daughter Edith who married Sir James Fergusson of Kilkerran. Ultimately their daughter Susan Georgiana succeeded to the estate and is the present owner. She married the late J. G. A. Baird of Wellwood, Ayrshire, who was M.P. for the central district of his county from 1886 till 1906.

The family of Broun is of great antiquity, the earliest known ancestor being Walter le Brun, who lived about 1120. The estate has descended in direct line, male or female, from Sir David Broun, whose name appears in a charter of date 1272—with one change when it went by sale to one of the same family under very remarkable circumstances. And these circumstances introduce the fascinating legend of " The Lady and the Pear." There were really two ladies of the pear, with an interval of a few hundred years.

The former was a daughter of Sir Hugo de Gifford, a baron and a wizard of the thirteenth century, whose name survives in the village of Gifford, and whose castle is still represented by a beautiful ruin of which the most important part, known as the " Goblin Hall," was built by spirits under his control. I have been in it. And Sir Walter Scott, the " Wizard of the North," described its building in " Marmion," canto iii., stanza 19. Sir Hugo had a daughter who married a Brun. As the bridal party proceeded to the church, Sir Hugo plucked a pear off a tree and gave it to his daughter, at the same time warning her to keep it carefully and to hand it on to her family, with the promise that as long as the family kept it carefully and safely prosperity would accompany them. And it is the case that the family did prosper.

And the Colstoun Pear is a reality, for I have seen it, or rather what remains of it—under suitable safeguards against my eating it. It is small and roundish, and looks very hard and unappetising— with a small piece missing; and that introduces us to the second lady, the Lady Elizabeth Mackenzie, daughter of the first Earl of Cromarty.   Her portrait by Sir John de Medina hangs in the dining-room.   She was the wife of Sir George Broun, the second baronet, at the beginning of the eighteenth century.

With her Highland blood she ought to have known better than to do it; but she bit a piece off the pear—which says much for her teeth.   And that broke the spell, so that soon part of the estate went to a bondholder.   And that was signified by the piece bitten off the pear.   Then her husband sold Colstoun to his brother Robert, thus separating the estate from the baronetcy.   Robert and his two sons were drowned, and the estate passed to his daughter Jean, who married her cousin Charles Broun, the grandfather of Charles of the Dean's story.   And the rest of the record has already been told.

XVIII

CRAIGCROOK CASTLE, CRAMOND, MIDLOTHIAN

CRAIGCROOK CASTLE was leased in November, 1874, by Robert Croall, a well-known citizen of Edinburgh, and occupied in March, 1875. From that time until now it has been occupied by his family, and is so still. It has been an inhabited house since the beginning of its existence, and has been intimately connected with the history and the great personages of Edinburgh.

There is a deep modern interest in it, for it was the country residence of Lord Jeffrey, Scottish judge and eminent literary man, from the year 1815 until his death in 1850; and in this house gathered from time to time all the great Whig lights of the first half of the nineteenth century—and some who were not Whigs. Sydney Smith, Brougham, Francis Horner, Lord Macaulay, Lord Cockburn, Sir Walter Scott, Professor Pillans, and many other ornaments of the literary world were entertained here, and their memories still haunt it. Indeed, I have heard it stated that the spirit of Jeffrey resides in it more than metaphorically.

Besides this modern interest there is also that of age. The date over the old gateway into the courtyard, still standing at the east end of the house, is 1626. That is the earliest inscribed date, but it is known that the building came into being in 1545, when it was a "keep" for the defence and provisioning of Edinburgh in the event of siege.

The lands of Craigcrook have a longer history than the house. In the fourteenth century they were held by the family of Graham, as shown by a deed of date April 9, 1362, by which Patrick and David Graham made them over to John de Alyncrum, a burgess of Edinburgh. He settled the lands or their income on a chaplaincy of the church of St. Giles, in Edinburgh, that masses might be said for the souls of all the kings and queens of Scotland, past and future, similarly the burghers of Edinburgh, many others specified, and, lastly, all the faithful departed. The rental at the time was £6 6s. 8d. Scots, equal to 10s. 8d. sterling, so the good man expected a good deal for his money.

When the proceeds were not further wanted for masses, Sir Simon Preston, of Craigmillar, Provost of Edinburgh, made over the lands to Sir Edward Marjoribanks, who was styled Prebend of Craigcrook. He let the lands for a year to George Kirkaldy, brother of Sir James Kirkaldy, of Grange ; but in 1542 he assigned them in feu farm to William Adamson, a burgess of Edinburgh, known from that time as " Adamson of Craigcrook." He is believed to have been a son of that Bailie Adamson who was one of the guardians of Edinburgh after Flodden, and was himself killed at Pinkie in 1547.

It is believed that Adamson built the castle, and the shield above the courtyard gate is supposed to bear his arms; but the date 1626 is too late for him, and it may be that of a descendant. At first the house was small, a rectangle about 35 feet by 20, and it is thought that its shape was that of the letter Z, roughly, with a total length of 50 feet. That means that it had a line in the main block 35 feet from west to east, with a round tower on the south-west corner and a square tower at the north-east. The entrance was in the square tower, and the north front was the principal front, as it is now after many alterations. The round tower is still there, about 22 feet in diameter, but the other is absorbed in the interior of the house, and was probably 16 feet square. The Adamsons added to the building in 1626, when Walter was the owner; and the additions practically doubled the old line, while leaving the width unchanged.

About 1656 the house passed into the hands of John Muir, an Edinburgh merchant, who probably altered the wall around the house, as a gateway in it has the date 1662. John Muir sold the property to Sir John Hall, Lord Provost of Edinburgh from 1689 till 1692, and a baronet of date 1687. When Hall obtained the estate of Dunglass he sold Craigcrook to Walter Pringle, an advocate, who sold it to John Strachan, Clerk to the Signet. Strachan left the property on his death to charitable purposes under the name of " the Craigcrook Mortification," and the place was let in 1736 on a ninety-nine years' lease, of which Archibald Constable, the publisher, took over the later period in the early part of the nineteenth century. He is said to have " made great improvements in the mansion and grounds," and " rendered it partly the commodious modern residence which Lord Jeffrey found it for so many summers of his life."

When Jeffrey first occupied it in 1815 he wrote to his father-in-law, Charles Wilkes, describing it as " an old manor house, 18 feet wide and 50 feet long, with irregular projections of all sorts, three staircases, turrets, and a large round tower at one end, with a multitude of windows of all sorts and sizes." Clerk of Eldin had made an etching of the south front in 1770, and it shows the " large round

CRAIGCROOK CASTLE
THE SOUTH FRONT, WITH THE
OLD TOWER AT THE SOUTH-WEST ANGLE

CRAIGCROOK CASTLE
THE SOUTH FRONT, LOOKING WEST

tower," but without the turret rising from it now so conspicuously. The lease expired in 1835, and the house came more directly into Jeffrey's hands, while in that year he made some alterations. The Croall family have made some changes, but have not altered the main features.

Jeffrey's architect was William H. Playfair, whose greatest alterations were on the north front. He added to the old rectangle an extension practically square, with a gable facing north and crow-stepped on the inner side. A flight of very handsome steps leads up at an angle to the face, with a classical balustrade, Crow-stepped gables, pediments, and dormer windows are the predominant notes of Playfair's work here and in his extension to the east; but the south front remains the front of beauty, standing today practically as it emerged from Jeffrey's reconstruction, which preserved the old features, as is seen from a comparison with Clerk of Eldin's etching.

The interior has many memorials of Jeffrey. That which brings us into more immediate contact with the shade of Jeffrey is his small round library in the big round tower. It opens off the morning-room, which occupies the whole area of the oldest house. The morning-room was the principal sitting-room in Jeffrey's day. There is a painting done on the east wall, which probably will never be disturbed, for it is a memorial of a remarkable personality of Jeffrey's time — David Roberts, the house painter, scene painter, and landscape painter, son of a shoemaker in the Stockbridge district of Edinburgh. He began his artistic career by drawing on the whitewashed walls of his father's house with red keel and the burnt ends of matches, and he became a Royal Academician.

The judge's library contains one of the famous heads of Stirling Castle, carved on wood medallions. The associations of the room are symbolised by photographs and prints of Sir Walter Scott, Sydney Smith, Macaulay, Tennyson, Carlyle, Cockburn, and other literary lions, many of whom had been entertained in these very rooms. The room is rather dark, owing to its wood lining and its ceiling of ribbed wood. A few years ago an old staircase was discovered at the joining of the round room with the west face—probably the relic of a small corbelled-out turret.

Every old house is a House of Shades, Craigcrook superlatively so, and the dominant shade is Jeffrey's. Cockburn his biographer surrounds him with his companion Shades, and Cockburn is one of them. Those two began with rugged Scottish accents at a time when gentlefolks were parting with it. Cockburn kept his and was proud of it; Jeffrey was not—and tried to get rid of it. He only succeeded in attaining what is still known as " high English " at the Scottish Bar. It reaches the House of Commons occasionally, and is both a puzzle and an amusement.

Jeffrey's critical writings had a terrible bite in them, and he bit Lord Byron, who then bit Jeffrey in " English Bards and Scotch Reviewers."

> " The Tolbooth felt defrauded of his charms
> If Jeffrey died except within her arms—
> Then prosper, Jeffrey, pertest of the train
> Whom Scotland pampers with her fiery grain ;
> Health to immortal Jeffrey ; once in name
> England could boast a Judge almost the same ;
> In soul so like, so merciful, so just,
> Some think that Satan has resigned his trust,
> And given the spirit to the world again,
> To sentence letters as he sentenced men."

XIX

CRAUFURDLAND CASTLE, KILMARNOCK, AYRSHIRE

THE distance of Craufurdland Castle from Kilmarnock is barely three miles by road, almost due north from the town. There is great variety in the scenery of Ayrshire, which is inferior to few counties of Scotland in the beauty of its landscape, although it is hardly known to fame as a scenic locality. The band of low ground which borders the shores of the Firth of Clyde is seldom more than four or five miles broad, except when it forms the valley of a river. From this belt the ground rises to the interior until it reaches a level of more than 1,000 feet above the sea, and from that level spring many peaks, some of them well over 2,000 feet in height. This continues to be the character of the land through the southern part of Lanarkshire and through Dumfriesshire

The parish of Kilmarnock is within the widest part of the coastal belt, in the watershed of the River Irvine. The name indicates a very old parish, the *cille* or holy cell of St. Marnoch, who was doubtless one of the band of early Scoto-Irish missionaries prepared for their work at Iona.

In this parish the Craufurds of Craufurdland have one of the oldest settlements, for they trace to Sir Reginald de Craufurd, Sheriff of Ayr, who lived about the beginning of the thirteenth century, and married the heiress of Loudoun. There are different accounts of the process by which John Craufurd, the first laird, came into possession of that estate of Craufurdland, but there is no doubt that he lived in the reign of Alexander II., was grandson of Sir Reginald, and handed on his Craufurdland property, previously called Ardoch, to his eldest son John. The tradition of the locality is that the castle was built in the eleventh century. The situation is full of beauty, the grounds extensive and finely wooded, and the house overhanging the Craufurdland Water.

The principal front faces the north-west, and is an imposing structure built in the Gothic style, that front dating from about 100 years ago. There is a fine Gothic entrance, with a coat of arms on a panel above it, and a splendid window of ecclesiastical appearance above that. These belong to a great central tower with

73

corbelled battlements and little round turrets. To the left is a small wing of a different style, with a crow-stepped gable to the front. This low part was added in 1648.

To the right of the central block is the most interesting part of the whole edifice, the old tower, now forming the west end of the castle. Just how old it is even an experienced architect would have difficulty in saying. It is very plain, solid, and strong, with only three windows in it, and they are evidently not of the same age as the wall. There is a battlemented top with rounded angles and a plain corbelling of four courses girdling it. Above this is a roof with crow-stepped gables, and still higher is the cape-house over the staircase, finished with crow-stepped gablets. The basement is provided with shot-holes. A well-known architectural work attributes it to a date about 1550; but a comparison with the part built in 1648, about the date of which there is no doubt, since it has the year carved on it, gives the impression that it must be at least a couple of centuries earlier than 1550.

The interior of the house has its age characteristics well preserved. There is an entrance-hall with plenty of width but a comparatively low ceiling. It extends to the right into the old tower, on the ground floor of which is the billiard-room looking out to the south, which is the back of the house, with its charming view of the valley of the Craufurdland Water. On the front are cellars and storage rooms with the grand old vaulted ceilings of bare stone which are so greatly valued now. Doubtless these particular vaulted rooms will receive greater honour in time than their present useful but humble purposes give them.

From the hall, between the billiard-room and the vaulted rooms, rises the staircase. On the first floor there are all the delights of a real old house. The drawing-room faces the south. To the east runs a long passage leading to various rooms, while on the north side are the dining-room and two passages. In the drawing-room is a beautiful piece of landscape tapestry covering the wall at one end, while the dining-room has a character all its own—a remarkably high ceiling and doors with pointed Gothic tops.

There was always a very close friendship between the families of Craufurd of Craufurdland and Boyd of Kilmarnock. Two stories of this friendship exist, one of them certainly true and the other perhaps an invention. Let the invention come first.

The ancient seat of the Boyds, Earls of Kilmarnock, was about two miles from Craufurdland on the way to Kilmarnock and had the name Dean Castle. An underground passage connected the two houses, and was only built up when the new Gothic front of Crau-

CRAUFURDLAND CASTLE
THE MAIN FRONT

CRAUFURDLAND CASTLE
THE OLD TOWER
AT THE WEST END

furdland was raised. The soldiers of Edward I. of England sat round Dean Castle three months in an effort to starve it. When they themselves were suffering from want of food they were surprised to see the garrison hang out a great show of fresh beef from the battlements. At the same time the garrison offered some to the besiegers, saying that they had more than they could use. So the disgusted commander at once raised the siege. It was the underground passage that had done it.

At this point the cold-blooded historian comes in and explains that the Boyds did not possess this castle of Dean until after Bannockburn, when it was conferred on them by King Robert Bruce on the forfeiture of its previous owner, John de Baliol.

The true story is one of faithful friendship. John Walkinshaw Craufurd of Craufurdland served in the army in the reigns of George II. and George III. He was a friend of the last Earl of Kilmarnock, who was executed for his share in the " 'forty-five." He is said to have held a corner of the cloth which received the head of the unfortunate nobleman; and he performed the last act of friendship by arranging for the proper burial of the body. As a result he was put at the bottom of the Army list; but he distinguished himself on service, and was made Falconer to the King in Scotland in 1761, ultimately becoming Lieutenant-Colonel. He died in 1793, having on his death-bed settled his estate upon Thomas Coutts the banker. After long litigation this settlement was reduced, and the estate returned to the family in the person of Elizabeth Craufurd, who had married John Houison of Braehead, near Cramond, Midlothian. She was aunt of the Laird.

The estate was inherited from her by her only surviving child Elizabeth, heiress of both properties, who married the Reverend James Moodie. They took the two names of Houison and Craufurd. As owner of Braehead this lady inherited a very famous tradition which Sir Walter Scott related in his *Tales of a Grandfather*.

According to Sir Walter's account, James V., known in his nocturnal rambles as the " Gudeman of Ballengeich," was on one occasion attacked by vagrants or gipsies near Cramond Bridge. He defended himself valiantly on the narrow bridge, but was obliged to shout for help. A farmer's man, Jock Howieson, who was working in a neighbouring field, went to his aid and laid about him so lustily that the two beat off the assailants. Then Jock took the king, without any idea as to who he was, to his house, where he provided a basin, ewer, and towel, to wash off the blood of the fray. Sir Walter made quite a long story of it, the end being a visit of Jock to Holyrood and the granting to him of the farm on which he was working, which happened to be royal property, on the feudal tenure of repeating his former service when required.

This is the *servitium lavacri*, which Sir William Fraser, in *Memorials of the Earls of Haddington*, controverting the story, proved to have existed in the reign of James III. But Sir Walter was wrong as to the family tradition, which gives the king as James I. or James II.

The service was rendered to George IV. on his visit to Edinburgh in 1822; and again it was rendered to George V., this time at Holyrood, on July 13, 1927, by Brigadier-General Houison-Craufurd.

XX

CULZEAN CASTLE, MAYBOLE, AYRSHIRE

CULZEAN CASTLE stands in a truly magnificent position on the coast of Ayrshire, perched on the top of the cliffs which contain the famous "Coves of Culzean," the haunt of smugglers in days which are not very long past. From the surface of the water at high tide to the top of the rock is about 100 feet. The present castle was founded by David Earl of Cassillis in the year 1777, but it had at least two predecessors, of which one was built by Sir Thomas Kennedy, who was murdered in 1602. There is no external trace of the building which existed before that period, but its site and the old tower are incorporated in the present building. It was in the very old days a secondary possession of the family of the Kennedys, which had its chief seat at Dunure Castle; but Culzean was nearly as old as the venerable Dunure, and Dunure still exists as a hoary ruin not very far away.

The present Culzean is the work of Robert Adam, and stands in a demesne of 700 acres containing beautiful trees, gardens, and an imposing pond which has the dimensions of a lake. As we approach the castle by the principal avenue, which rises as we advance, the first glimpse of the house is obtained at a bend towards the left. This view is very striking, with its three garden terraces on the south-east frontage. The building is often described as Gothic, but it is hardly that in the ordinary sense of the term. Nor is it in the Scottish classical style which the Adams made so popular. It is rather an adaptation of Roman and baronial styles, combined with wonderful skill and beauty. There is a multiplicity of round towers, springing from their own foundations, with here and there a rectangular tower or tower face, as at the north angle facing the sea. There are occasional features of the Tudor Gothic style, as in the large bay with mullioned and transomed windows in the south front of the west wing, now known as the "New Wing," having been rebuilt by the present Marquis of Ailsa in 1879. The arches are all semicircular in the Roman style, and the walls are in every case surmounted by a battlemented parapet in the baronial style.

Passing the bend of the avenue we come in sight of a handsome gateway and arch leading into the courtyard. A prominent feature

77

is the great square flag-tower to the east of the main buildings, and on the most precipitous part of the cliffs. It is of great height, and contains a clock. A pathway close to the base of the tower leads down to the beach, where we can obtain an impressive view of much of the building. We see the handsome open classical balustrade which runs in front of the first floor of the flag-tower, guarding the balcony of the " round drawing-room," from which a magnificent picture is obtained of the setting sun colouring the distant hills of Arran, and striking on the lofty mass of Ailsa Craig, fifteen miles away.

The entrance porch stands slightly in advance of the east front. By it we enter the outer hall, an oblong room with its greater length from west to east. Moving forward to the west, we pass through a central doorway into an inner hall which is known as the " armoury " Still proceeding west, we enter a great oval hall named the " circle," from which rises the grand staircase to our left on the north side. The oval is bounded by great columns, on the outer side of which runs a passage all the way round. On the south side of the passage are two large rooms, of which the nearer, formerly the dining-room, has been the library since 1879, while the further is the dining-room. Other rooms lead off this passage all the way round.

The stair which leads to the first floor emerges on another oval, from which ascend two stairs to the upper rooms on a third oval. On the first floor is the beautiful " round drawing-room." On the south side of the oval on this floor is a series of three charming rooms overlooking the terraces on the main front, the middle room of the three being the " long drawing-room."

The Marquis of Ailsa, owner of this delightful castle, is an experienced sailor and holds the certificate of a master-mariner. His bent is illustrated in various parts of the house, where models of seacraft are to be found. In the outer hall many length-sections of yachts indicate their lines, one on the right being a model of the cutter yacht *Cocker*, five tons, designed by the Marquis and built at the Culzean Yacht and Steam Launch Works in 1880 and 1881. These works were established by the Marquis.

The armoury is fully described by its name, for it has a remarkable collection of ancient weapons. In addition, there stand in the centre of the room two tables with cases containing models of ships. One is that of a 68-ton frigate-built warship of the period of the early Georges, with the " lion " figurehead. The Marquis found it in an almost ruined state in the house of a relative, had it restored, and was presented with it. Many small brass cannon stand on the uncarpeted stone floor ; and two mortars for throwing grenades,

CULZEAN CASTLE
THE SOUTH FRONT

CULZEAN CASTLE
LOOKING SOUTH-WEST
FROM THE SEA

used at the siege of Badajos in the Peninsular War, are near the fireplace.

In ascending the grand staircase we are struck by the dignity and beauty of the great open space or " well " round which all the rooms are arranged, and it is surmounted by a brilliantly lighted cupola. Many pictures of historical personages are in various rooms, one of the most interesting being a painting of Mary Queen of Scots, which hangs in the boudoir of the Marchioness. The story attached to it is that it is one of those given to the families of the eight Commissioners sent to France in 1557 to negotiate the marriage of Mary with the Dauphin. They stood out against giving the Dauphin the " Crown Matrimonial " of Scotland; and four of them, including Gilbert, third Earl of Cassillis, died in 1558 on their way home, it is supposed by poison. The portrait ought to be regarded as a good likeness of Queen Mary.

The Marquis of Ailsa is the head of the family of Kennedy, and his older title of Earl of Cassillis is borne by his eldest son. The name Kennedy is in the Gaelic " Ceannadach," and apparently indicates headship, with the inference that the family inherited an old headship of the Pictish kingdom or province of Galloway, in the southwest of Scotland.

Fergus, Prince of Galloway, died in 1161 and left two sons, Uchtred and Gilbert, and his immediate descendants took " De Carrick " as their name, from the district of their lands. The next stage in development is the Earldom of Carrick, and then we come to a time when Marjory, Countess of Carrick, held the earldom in her own right. In 1271 she was a widow when she met Robert Bruce, son of the Earl of Annandale, hunting in her demesne; and she took him more or less forcibly to her castle of Turnberry, where she married him without consulting king or relations, and he thus became Earl of Carrick in his wife's name.

But he could not take the " kenkynol " or chieftainship of the clan of Kennedy, which went to Gilbert, who appears to have been an ancestor of John Kennedy of Dunure, to whom Robert II. confirmed an old charter of the " kenkynol " and the bailiery of Carrick with the leading of its men. The date is 1372.

A Gilbert Kennedy of Dunure was made Lord Kennedy in 1457, and his grandson became Earl of Cassillis in 1509 and was among those killed at Flodden in 1513. Archibald, the 12th Earl, was made Marquis of Ailsa in 1831; and the present Marquis is the third of that creation. There have been in the succession, apart from the original lairds, two Lords Kennedy, eleven Earls, and three Marquises—a goodly line of sixteen holders of the original title.

79

One of them, James, married the Princess Mary, daughter of Robert III.

The family of Kennedy has produced many turbulent men, and many pious men and women. One of the pious men was William, Abbot of Crossraguel; and his successor was another Kennedy, Quinton, who held a debate with John Knox at Maybole. Quinton was succeeded by a Stewart, which so annoyed Quinton's nephew Gilbert, the 4th Earl, known as the "King of Carrick," that he seized the new Abbot, took him to the "Black Vaut of Dunure," and held him before a slow fire until he was ready to sign away what the Earl wanted.

The reason of the action was this. Abbot Kennedy, who was a real abbot, had given the Earl a twenty years' "tack," or lease, of certain Abbey lands, and ten years had still to run. But Abbot Alan Stewart, who was only an imitation abbot, leased the lands to another tenant at a higher rent, thus looking for trouble. And he found it.

The name "Culzean" is pronounced "Cul-lane," with the accent on the second syllable.

XXI

DALMAHOY HOUSE, RATHO, MIDLOTHIAN

THE records of the Dalmahoy estate carry back to the days of King Alexander III., and, although Dalmahoy House and estate are in the parish of Ratho, it is probable that the barony of Dalmahoy is as old as that of Ratho. The two baronies existed side by side for many centuries, and only three families seem to have held Dalmahoy—the Dalmahoys, a Dalrymple, and the family of the Earl of Morton, who is the present owner.

Alexander Nisbet's famous *System of Heraldry*, of date 1722, and a recent work on the plates which he intended to use either for that or another work, and which were only rediscovered a few years ago, give the names of the generations of owners fairly fully. The first of the line known was Sir Alexander de Dalmahoy, who granted permission to the monks of Newbattle in 1265 to pass through his lands. His son was Sir Henry de Dalmahoy, who lived in the time of Alexander III. and submitted to Edward I. of England in 1296. He must have joined the winning side later, as the family retained the estate.

The date of the present house is about the year 1710, judging from references which do not give the precise date. Three heraldic emblazonments represent the three families. That of the Dalmahoys is on a wall in the stable yard; the other two are to be found close together on the west front, which is now the entrance-front, although it may be assumed as possible that the first entrance was on the east front, where there is a charming double flight of steps leading to a doorway with a finely sculptured emblazonment above it.

The other two emblazonments are associated with a fine porch on the west front. It is built out 16 feet in front of the line of its block and is about 18 feet wide. An open classical balustrade encloses the roof of the porch, and in the centre of the front of the balustrade a large stone panel carries the arms of the House of Douglas with supporters, all in full relief. The porch must have been built since the house came into the possession of the family of Douglas in 1760.

Just above the porch is the window of the dining-room; and the window has above it a wide cornice supporting a very elaborate

81   G

heraldic sculpture, which on examination shows two coats of arms, perhaps impaled. One part indicates the Dalrymple family, and the other looks like the shield of Hope of Balcomy as shown in Nisbet's book, while the motto " Firm " is that of the Dalrymples. Doubtless the Dalrymple who bought the property in 1720 from the Dalmahoys put up the device to mark his possession ; but it is possible that he built or altered that west front.

The main design of the whole house is that of a rectangular block, the east face symmetrical, but with a lower part to the north which is evidently later. All fronts show three storeys, the east front having narrow projecting wings, and the west front a wide projecting centre, with octagonal towers at the outside angles, surmounted by octagonal tapering roofs. The east face is plastered rought-cast, with the corners of rustic masonry, and plain string-courses run above and below the middle storey. An open parapet of classical balusters is above the east face, with the usual urn ornament at intervals, and a similar arrangement is found on the west front; but on the north and south ends the parapet is solid.

These features, and those mentioned in connection with the emblazonments, give material for conjecture as to the architect who designed the house. Judged by the style, it seems to mark almost a complete breakaway from the old Scottish style of domestic building. It shows a strong resemblance to the outstanding features of Kinross House, the work of Sir William Bruce, although it is smaller and less rich in its architectural scheme. But Sir William Bruce died in 1710—the year in which it is assumed that the house was built. However, Bruce's style was carried on by his pupil William Adam, who lived till 1748 ; and William Adam left his style to be fully developed by his two more famous sons. It looks as if Dalmahoy House is the work of William Adam.

The present entrance is by the porch on the west front, and it leads into a plain outer hall, with doorways right and left into the octagonal towers. Then comes a large inner hall, and after that another inner hall, from which rises the great stair on our left. Beyond that is the library, which looks out from the east front. There is accordingly by this series of rooms a complete passage from one front to the other. To the south are passages, another stair, bedrooms, and the oak room, which has an entrance off the library. There is nothing especially distinctive in the arrangement or furnishings of these rooms.

When we ascend the great stair we see a large painting, by Davison, of the 16th Earl of Morton and his first wife, Agatha Haliburton, with their family, facing us as we arrive at the drawing-

DALMAHOY HOUSE
FROM THE SOUTH-EAST

DALMAHOY HOUSE
FROM THE SOUTH-WEST

room landing. The dining-room is on the west side. The drawing-room is of impressive dimensions. The interest of the interior is chiefly to be found in historical paintings.

On the east wall of the dining-room hangs a Raeburn portrait of the 17th Earl of Morton. The south wall of the drawing-room has a painting which purports to be a portrait of Sholto Douglas, an alleged founder of the family. But no reliance is to be placed upon this, especially as the name Sholto does not occur in the family until the fifteenth century. The first recorded member of the family is William de Douglas, of somewhere about the year 1174; and the family was then great. On the west wall is a portrait of peculiar interest, that of William, the 7th Earl, who was Lord High Treasurer of Scotland. He was born in 1582, and was a son of the Douglas of Lochleven who was the custodian of Queen Mary in the castle of Lochleven.

One of the famous paintings of the family possession has recently gone to the Municipal Art Gallery at Glasgow, that of Mary Queen of Scots, while a kind of companion picture, that of the Regent Morton, remains. Queen Mary used to hang in the drawing-room, and the constant tradition is that it was given by the Queen to George Douglas when she was confined in Lochleven Castle under his father's or his mother's wardship. George was sent away from the castle because he was known to be in love with Mary, and had already been concocting a plan for her liberation. But he had left behind him another Douglas, a youth of eighteen years named William, of whom the rather virulent church historian Calderwood wrote that he was " called the laird's bastard brother, but in truth a foundling and no Dowglas." William accomplished the escape and threw the keys of the castle into the loch.

A writer in the *New Statistical Account of Scotland*—date 1839—recorded that " a few years ago," during a partial draining of the loch, a bunch of keys was found which were believed to be the old castle keys, and which were presented to the Earl of Morton. The present Earl is a descendant of the custodian and now has those keys.

The portrait is supposed to be the best of those of Queen Mary, and some years ago I found a statement that it was by Lucas de Heere. But on having occasion at a later date to trace the reference I could not find it.

The portrait of the Regent Morton, the 4th Earl, is well known. It is a three-quarter length, and the subject is apparently sitting at a table on which rest his gloves. He has a full beard and wears a sugar-loaf hat. His features do not by any means bear out the reputation for hardness and cruelty which has been handed down to us.

The " Dalmahoy Hangings " are of great interest, and a full description of them is to be found in the *Proceedings* of the Society of Antiquaries of Scotland, vol. lii., put before the Society in an account by R. Scott Moncrieff in February, 1918. They are often called tapestries, but they are not technically tapestries, and are said to have been worked by the Maries of the Queen during her imprisonment at Lochleven in 1567 and 1568.

XXII

DALZELL HOUSE, MOTHERWELL, LANARKSHIRE

DALZELL HOUSE is an example of a beautiful house in beautiful surroundings standing on the edge of a town which is a visible symbol of things which are not beautiful. That is, its main entrance is practically in the principal street of Motherwell. And the mere mention of Motherwell calls up visions of the Lanarkshire coalfield, with its huge smoke-stacks, its accumulations of refuse from below, and its smoke pall. Yet the area of the Lanarkshire coalfield is no " Black Country," in spite of the occasional blots upon the scenery thus enumerated.

We are not long inside the gates of Dalzell House before we are delighted with the beauty of the grounds. An avenue of about a mile in length leads up to the house through a wide-spreading park. And then the house itself is a revelation. It fulfils in itself all the characteristics which entitle a house to be called a castle. It has been in its day a real place of strength, and it is at present a splendid example of the possibility of adapting an ancient stronghold to the needs of modern comfort, by judicious addition and adaptation.

There is an ancient "keep"; there are the remains of a moat; the castle is perched upon an eminence. What more does a stronghold want, except the men for its defence and the weapons with which to arm them ?

On arriving at the house we find ourselves faced by a wall with a crenellated parapet; but it does not surround the building. It forms only a portion of the western side of the whole block, the wings of the house extending on each side of it. The wall is in keeping with the age of the oldest part, and, although considerably altered, may be regarded as essentially a part of the original wall which surrounded the castle. It has two wide entrances, with flat arches, leading into a courtyard; and the moat is bridged in front of each. The courtyard is paved and consists of a carriage-drive which, with the walls, encloses a space paved with large flat slabs. In front of us, when we have entered the courtyard, stands the central part of the house, the ancient "keep," rising to a height of 48 feet to the crenellated parapet on two rows of corbels. It is 39 feet long and

32 broad, so that even when it stood alone—if it ever did stand entirely by itself—it must have been quite impressive. This part is assigned to the middle of the fifteenth century, so that it is well on towards 500 years old.

The courtyard has the " keep " in the centre of its east side, with other buildings completing that side. On the south side is a later wing, belonging to the seventeenth century. But there is good reason to believe that the builders of this wing made use of some previous stone structure, for it contains an old vaulted kitchen, and the old keep did not originally have a kitchen, which is curious. The keep must have stood by itself, a large kitchen being a little distance from it as an independent building. When the south wing was built in the seventeenth century it must have been built on the site of this kitchen and included it. The keep has an unusual projection at the south-west angle, like a flat buttress of a Norman donjon. The old building had its chief entrance here, the grooves for the portcullis still visible, and doubtless there was a room above for working the portcullis.

As we face the keep, looking at its western side, there is a handsome entrance, cut through the wall in 1857 by R. W. Billing, the architect who designed the north wing. The doorway admits to a handsome vaulted hall, forming the basement of the tower. A window has been cut in the thickness of the east wall and is deeply splayed. The inner measurement across is 6 feet, while the outer width is only 1 foot 9 inches, and the depth of the recess is 6 feet 6 inches to the glass, with about 18 inches outside. On each side of the window stands a figure in ancient plate armour. On our left is a door which leads to the rooms in the modern north wing, while a door on the right opens upon stairs which go up in a round tower to the drawing-room and library in the south wing, and down to the old vaulted kitchen, which is now a billiard-room.

The dining-hall is above the entrance-hall and shares many of the characteristics of that room. As originally constructed it formed part of the vaulted basement, which was two storeys in height and had stone corbels in the walls some way up, with a floor supported by them. Above the narrow and widely splayed window of the entrance-hall, the dining-hall has a corresponding window in the thickness of the east wall; but it has been made of full size with hardly any splay. On the opposite side is a very handsome fireplace, wide and high, surmounted by shields, swords, halberds, battle-axes, and pieces of defensive armour. On the same side, high up in the wall, are two windows with arched tops, broken through the 8-feet thickness of the wall. The room is lined more than half-way to the

DALZELL HOUSE
THE WEST FRONT

DALZELL HOUSE
VIEW FROM THE DALZELL BURN; THE OLD KEEP
IN THE CENTRE

vaulted ceiling with beautifully carved oak panelling, and above the panelling are family portraits, with many specimens of ancient weapons. A specially interesting painting is that of Sir John Hamilton of Orbiston, who died in 1664, and is represented in armour.

The same stair leads to the drawing-room in the addition of the seventeenth century—an unusually handsome room, in which architecture, decorations, and furnishings combine to make a complete harmony. It also is lined with oak panelling, and is divided into two by two pairs of elaborately carved oak columns, highly polished. The plaster ceiling is of most ornate design and was executed by the architect, Mr. Billing, with his own hands. The room is lighted on the west and south, and the columns divide it into east and west rooms.

The east room has a very fine window, which was built in the alterations and restoration of the three years beginning with 1857. It is a large bay window without a foundation. The architect boldly threw out corbels from the wall, tier upon tier, each tier projecting further than that beneath it, until he had arranged five tiers. The corbelled supports carry beautifully mullioned windows which overlook the garden terraces, other windows being above them in the flatness of the wall of a great projecting bay, which rises to a crow-stepped gable.

As seen from the avenue which leads to the house in almost a straight line, the mass of masonry is impressive ; but the other views rival this. The Dalzell Burn flows behind in a deep ravine with many curves, eating away the soft material of the bed and shaping off a high and rugged eminence on which the castle stands. According to all the laws of mechanics, the building ought to have slipped down into the stream some hundreds of years ago, for it rests upon a bed of clay into which the foundations were roughly dug. This was discovered when the architect dug out the soil under the keep, to give height to the vaulted entrance hall; and he had to underbuild, so that if the house was not safe before, at any rate it is now.

On the south the garden terraces are a feature, overlooked by Billing's window, and numbering three on the slopes of the ravine, one below another, so arranged as all to be bathed in the midday sun—when it shines. A descent to the river bed, where I viewed the old modernised stronghold from a rocky slab in the midst of the water, was more than worth the trouble.

The owner, Lord Hamilton of Dalzell, is well known. The first of his family was John Hamilon, who acquired the estate of Orbiston in 1468, and was descended from Sir James Hamilton of Cadzow, father of the first Lord Hamilton and ancestor also of the Dukes of Hamilton and Abercorn. Dalzell Castle was originally the possession of the Dalzells, Lords of the Barony from the thirteenth century. It came to the Hamiltons through James Hamilton of Boggs, who bought it from Lord Dalzell, Earl of Carnwath, and was a nephew of the Earl through his mother, Christian, a daughter of Robert Dalzell of Dalzell.

XXIII

DOUGLAS CASTLE, DOUGLAS, LANARKSHIRE

AT Douglas Castle we are on historic ground in the country of
the doughty Douglases. There is an interesting and pretty
village of Douglas in the hill country of Lanarkshire, situated
on the Douglas water, where the level is between 700 and 800 feet
above the sea. A little further into the hill country is Douglas
Castle, in a grand and extensive demesne.

As the origin of the Douglas family is lost in antiquity, so is the
date of the first Douglas Castle. A traditional and romantic story is
related by Hume of Godscroft in his *History of the House of Douglas*,
first published in 1644—that in the year 767 Donald Bane was
warring against Salvathius, king of the Scots, and was almost victor,
when suddenly the king received valiant help from a man and his
sons, and was able to turn threatened defeat into notable victory.
The king asked who his helper was, and received for answer—" Sholto
Dhu-glas ": " There is the dark man." This, of course, is mere myth,
and its Gaelic will not stand examination. It is believed, however,
that the family is found in the days of King David I., whose reign
began in 1124. They appear in many events up to the time of the
Scottish War of Independence, when Sir William Douglas was one
of Wallace's supporters. Sir William's son was the " good Lord
James," friend and supporter of King Robert Bruce.

This intrepid man made it so difficult for the English to hold
his castle, which he could not hold against them, that it came to
be known as " the perilous Castle of Douglas "; and that is the origin
of Sir Walter Scott's fine romance of *Castle Dangerous*. Sir John de
Walton was to defend the castle for a year and a day, all for the love
of a lady who had promised her hand on the completion of the task.
Finally the lady recalled him to her side; but just then the Douglas
ambushed and slew Sir John, on whose body was found the lady's
letter.

The main point is that during all these stormy periods there was a
Douglas Castle and there was a Douglas. But there is not a vestige
left of the old castle, which had so many vicissitudes. The beginning
of the present castle dates from the year 1757, two years after its

89

predecessor had been destroyed by fire. The only Duke of Douglas began it, but died in 1761, when followed the " Douglas Cause," a most sensational suit in which the heir Archibald, son of the Duke's sister Lady Jane by her marriage with Sir John Stewart, of Grantully, was opposed on the ground that he was not their child, but had been obtained in order to bar the true succession. In 1769 the claim of Archibald was sustained. He did not inherit the ducal title with the estates, but was created Baron Douglas in 1790.

The brothers Adam designed the present castle on a most ambitious scale, but only one wing was finished, requiring another wing and a front for its completion. Although incomplete, it is a massive pile. Sir Walter Scott, in his introduction to *Castle Dangerous*, says that the present castle only amounts to one-eighth of the Adam design; but a later account says one-fourth. Apparently it was intended to have a magnificent east front, with a wing to the north similar to that which is the actual castle at present. Presumably the west side would be occupied by a handsome wall.

The entrance is by a porch and hall on the east side, both later than the great block. To the right of the entrance is the chapel, which has an air of somewhat severe simplicity, combined with beauty. It has a marble altar, a triptych, a number of figures above it, and a vaulted roof, divided into pictured panels.

Not far from the chapel is a relic which some identify with " Harrie's Tower," which was part of the castle when Lord Clifford held it against the good Lord James; but the identification is mistaken, and the relic is now accepted as the remains of a tower belonging to the wall surrounding the house which was burned in 1755. With its great cleft from top to bottom of its three or four storeys it is a romantic object.

The interior features of the house are as impressive as those without. All the rooms are high and handsome, and they contain many interesting paintings. The dining-room has the Earl of Stafford, Henry Duke of Buccleuch, and George Duke of Montagu. The drawing-room, of which the prevailing tones are brown and gold, has a Raeburn of Archibald Douglas, the heir in the " Douglas Cause "; Lady Lucy Douglas by Gainsborough; and Margaret, Duchess of Douglas, by Sir Joshua Reynolds.

The general character of the architecture, and the massiveness of the contemplated scheme, can only be gauged by a view obtained from a little distance. The general appearance is that of a great battlemented block, of which the south front gives a good idea, with its octagonal tower in the centre presenting three full faces, and its great round towers standing up at the extremities of the line.

DOUGLAS CASTLE
FROM THE EAST, WITH
THE OLD TOWER ON THE RIGHT

DOUGLAS CASTLE
THE DRAWING-ROOM

DOUGLAS CASTLE, LANARKSHIRE

Gothic windows, ornate parapets, and on the east side square-headed windows with mullion and transom, present a dignified pile to the eye, while on the east side is a fine terrace with ornamental steps leading down to the gardens on the south side.

The title given to Baron Douglas in 1790 ended with his third son, the fourth holder. His daughter married the second and last Lord Montagu, and their daughter married the 11th Earl of Home—the name pronounced Hume. The late Earl, the 12th, was their son; the Douglas estates went to him, and he was created Baron Douglas in the Peerage of the United Kingdom. The present Earl, the 13th, is his son.

It was a Douglas who was Regent of Scotland when the Scots were defeated at Halidon Hill in 1333; it was a greater Douglas who was the Regent Morton in the days of Queen Mary; a Douglas it was who died in Spain in battle against the Moors when he was carrying King Robert Bruce's heart to the Holy Land; a Douglas was the lord of the old tower and estate of Whittingehame, the present Earl Balfour's place; a Douglas preceded the Buccleuch family at Dalkeith; a Douglas guarded Queen Mary at Lochleven; and a Douglas helped her to escape. Douglases are celebrated in Border ballads such as "The Battle of Otterburn" and "Chevy Chase." They are mostly sung in deeds of blood, but there is one who is sung in a ballad which combines the deed of blood with a tragic theme of love.

The title is "The Douglas Tragedy," as given in Sir Walter Scott's *Border Minstrelsy*. A farm of Blackhouse in Selkirkshire, with the remains of an old tower near, is generally given as the scene, in a wild and solitary glen through which flows a mountain torrent called the Douglas Burn. It was one of the most ancient of the Douglas estates, and the personages of the ballad cannot be identified. Like "The Gipsy Countess," the theme is common to many countries, and is known in Danish, Icelandic, Norse, and Swedish variants.

The Lady Margaret eloped with her lover from the tower, and was followed by her father and seven brothers, who brought the lover to bay, on the banks of the Douglas Burn. "Lord William" is the hero who fought and killed all his pursuers while the lady looked on; but he only survived long enough to take the lady to his mother's house. The form in which I know it has twenty four-line stanzas, of which only a few will suffice to give the general line—

    1. "'Rise up, rise up now, Lord Douglas,' she says,
      'And put on your armour so bright;
      Let it never be said that a daughter of thine
      Was married to a lord under night.

2. " ' Rise up, rise up, my seven bold sons,
      And put on your armour so bright ;
      And take better care of your youngest sister,
      For your eldest's awa' the last night.'

3. " He's mounted her on a milk-white steed,
      And himself on a dapple grey,
      With a bugelet horn hung down by his side,
      And lightly they rode away.

6. " She held his steed in her milk-white hand,
      And never shed one tear,
      Until that she saw her seven brothers fa',
      And her father hard fighting, who loved her so dear.

18. " Lord William was buried in St. Mary's kirk,
      Lady Marg'ret in Mary's quire ;
      Out o' the lady's grave grew a bonnie red rose,
      And out o' the knight's a brier.

19. " And they two met and they two plat,
      And fain they wad be near ;
      And a' the warld might ken right weel,
      They were two lovers dear.

20. " But by and rade the Black Douglas,
      And wow, but he was rough ;
      For he pull'd up the bonnie brier,
      And flang't it in St. Mary's Loch."

XXIV

DUNDAS CASTLE, SOUTH QUEENSFERRY, WEST LOTHIAN

WHEN we speak of Dundas Castle we may mean either of two houses—one ancient and the other modern, but the two so close in position and relationship that they may be taken as one. The old castle occupies a site which slopes rapidly down to the west, north-west, and south-west; and it is formed of two blocks at right angles to each other. Indications exist to suggest that there was a great fortified court, of which the castle was the keep, or " donjon." The unbroken fronts are to the north and west. There is not much doubt about the date of the building, for in 1416 a Dundas of Dundas received a warrant from Robert Duke of Albany, to erect a fortalice, while in 1424 a further warrant was granted by King James I. for an addition, which was doubtless the small block at the north-west angle.

This old castle was a finely built edifice. All the rooms are vaulted, and there are some fireplaces which charm the eye of the antiquarian. It has had a somewhat chequered career, and was even used as a distillery at the beginning of the nineteenth century, with traces yet of various structures of brick which conceal the beauties of the interior. On the outside it is a distinctly striking building. Seen from the rising ground to the south, it comes into line with the modern house, rising high above and behind the buildings which enclose the stable-yard, dwarfing by its height even the modern house, which has a very long frontage, and showing up strongly the contrast between a mighty frowning fortalice and a comfortable Gothic residence.

The date of the modern edifice is 1818, carved on a kind of bartizan at the north-west corner of the main front block. The builder was James Dundas, and his architect William Burn. Probably it was the architect's first really important work, and he was only twenty-nine years of age when he designed it. He built St. John's Church, Princes Street, Edinburgh, the same year, and did later work on Riccarton, Niddrie Marischal, and Tyninghame.

The simplest method of describing the modern house is to begin with a great rectangular space, in which the old castle has a very small area on the short western side, while the main house occupies the whole length of the eastern side, covering a considerable area. North, south, and much to the east, of the old castle is a courtyard; while to the east of the courtyard is a series of low-roofed buildings of different heights, bordering the main blocks. The main blocks have dignified Gothic frontages to south and east, the south front extending west until it joins the low buildings which enclose the stable yard, these buildings forming a great square. The principal front faces the south, and contains the main entrance, which is formed by a wide porch under a flattened Gothic arch. The buildings are only two storeys in height.

To left and right of the porch rise round towers with battlemented tops, that on the left close to the porch and the other separated from it by a Jacobean window of three lights. The part of the front to the left of the other round tower is divided into two sections by a buttress which rises higher than the roof. Between tower and buttress is an octagon window with three sides projecting. Mullions divide it into seven lights, it has a crenellated top, and has above it a very large Gothic window of ecclesiastical design and arched moulding. The other windows are of varied design. The east front is plainer, but is carried out on a similar design, varied by the centre part between two slender octagonal towers having a pedimented top. The pediment contains the Dundas arms, with supporters and crest, all carved with great clearness.

A few steps rise from the porch to admit to the square hall, which widens out to the left, where a passage runs westward. A little further within the house the grand staircase rises to the left. Still further on the hall is continued in a long corridor from south to north, the whole length of the east front. It is very striking, and so ecclesiastical in its style that it is sometimes described as a " cloister," which is not quite correct. It is entirely of oak, with a groined roof on excellent lines. The windows on the left are of coloured glass, and obtain their light from a small interior courtyard.

On the right of the hall is the drawing-room, not large, but very pleasing with its light colouring; and it has a plaster ceiling designed in intersecting curves. It is lighted on the east by three windows and on the south by the Jacobean window. Beyond it is the library, with a handsome oak fireplace, the overmantel supported on rounded columns of which the capitals are carved human faces. The dining-room follows the same line of the east front, and has a panelled ceiling similar in form to that of the library, and a fireplace also similar.

The fountain sundial is a unique feature which requires extended

DUNDAS CASTLE
THE OLD CASTLE
FROM THE SOUTH-WEST

DUNDAS CASTLE
THE SOUTH FRONT

notice. In the early part of the seventeenth century the enclosed court commanded by the old castle had banqueting houses at each of the angles. They are associated in this way with the fountain sundial that they were probably, as the sundial was with certainty, built by Sir Walter Dundas, the laird of the day. The story is that he found himself with enough money to buy the barony of Barn-bougle, and was greatly upset because the Earl of Haddington anticipated him. So he spent the money in the gorgeous arrange-ment of which the fountain sundial was the centre. The old court-yard must have been very charming then, with the walls, the angle banqueting rooms, and the magnificent structure occupying its centre.

The walls have gone, and the sundial has been removed to the east of the modern house, where it stands in a lawn slightly sunk, with steps descending to it. The platform of the sundial is ap-proached by nine steps, like those of an old " ramp," and may be described as square. It has evoked unrestrained admiration from numerous writers, and deserves it. There are two main ledges, on the upper of which stands the unique column which bears the dials, the ledges being for the fall and splash of the water. There is exquisite carving of many figures, some of them human, with architectural forms and graceful lines. And an elaborate Latin inscription runs round it in the upper and lower panels, in capital letters—an inscription so long that it must have been written by one who was proud of his Latinity in a day when scholars could converse in the language of the ancient Romans.

A moderately good Latinist of the present day would find it easy enough to reach the sense of the inscription, although he might not find it so easy to provide a literal translation. In it the visitor is exhorted to observe, read, study, and protect the stones through which the spring water is carried, in order that the thirsty garden may be moistened ; not to destroy ; and to quench his thirst in the year 1623 of man's salvation. The inscription goes on to tell that the fountain is under the protection of the castle, that it was built in the year 1623 by Sir Walter Dundas, and that it is surrounded by guardian spirits to frighten evil-doers. Friends and strangers are invited to make use of the gardens, the sundials, the fountain, and the cushions distributed on the seats. Apparently the courtyard was a show place in 1623.

The family of Dundas has always claimed to have sprung from the same progenitor as the old Earls of Dunbar, the first being Helias de Dundas, who received the lands from the Earl of Dunbar soon after the year 1100. From him have descended in the unbroken male line twenty-nine Dundases of that ilk. James, the twenty-sixth, who built the modern house, found himself involved in greater expense in that work than he anticipated. And other things went wrong too, so that in 1875 he sold the house and the greater part of the estate. Ultimately Mr. Stewart Clark of Cairndhu became the owner, and was succeeded by his only son, John Stewart Clark, who was created a baronet. Sir John's son, Sir Stewart Stewart-Clark, is the present baronet and laird.

XXV

HATTON HOUSE, RATHO, MIDLOTHIAN

HATTON HOUSE is the residence of William Whitelaw, chairman of the great combination of railways now bearing the name of the "London and North-Eastern Railway." It is a highly modernised house brought up to date without sacrificing the features and characteristics of a very ancient and remarkable house which has much history behind it.

Tall elms and spreading beeches are to be found in the avenue, with lime-trees and hollies, yews and rhododendrons—an avenue perhaps less than half a mile long, but probably the old and original approach. Hatton is merely the remainder of an old estate. When it was bought by the Earl of Morton in 1870 it comprised about 500 acres; but when the 8th Earl of Lauderdale sold it in 1792 it was nearer 2,000 acres of excellent land. The house has many entrances, but that in the east front is the chief. A walled-in terrace lies before it, approached by fourteen steps which lead up to the "Lion Gateway." Lions surmount the stone columns of rustic work, with handsome frieze and cornice, which carry the gate; and the two dates 1692 and 1829, with a sundial wrongly placed, attest that the position of the gateway was changed at the later date.

Next comes a court almost square, with a wall built by the present Laird on three sides and the other side the east front of the house. It is easy for anyone to see that it is a very old house, and yet its history and character are hardly known, even in its near neighbourhood, while an ordinary view does not suggest its actual age. It does not present to the eye the form of an ancient "keep," but the keep is there, a buried nucleus, which an examination of old records proclaims to be not later than some time between 1350 and 1450. On the east front a north wing and a south wing have the date 1664, the two-storeyed line between them having the date 1714. Behind this line is the old keep, with only the upper part visible, and that so modified by the breaking of windows in the walls as to conceal the age of the whole mass, with its classical balustrade and "lantern" roof-light covered by an ogee roof.

The south front has no indication of the keep, but consists of a central square block about 30 feet broad, projecting a few feet in front of the general line. There is a large round tower at each end of the south line, which has a total length of about 135 feet, as compared with the east line of 145 feet. On the east face of the south-east angle tower, close to the top window, is a sundial with the monogram " C.M.E.L.," which stands for Charles Maitland and his wife Elizabeth Lauder, the date 1664 being divided by the monogram. Charles Maitland became the 3rd Earl of Lauderdale, and built very fully round the keep on the east, south, and west sides. Another dial, at the west end, has the date 1675.

On the south front, over the extreme left dormer window, are the initials " C.M."; the middle dormer is left blank; the next has " E.L."; the first pediment to the right of the central block has the word "anno"; and the next has the date 1640. A prominent feature in the central block is a great panel containing the Lauder arms, supposed to have been removed from the old keep when the Maitlands made their great additions. In this same central part of the south front a small spiral staircase in the thickness of the wall was discovered in 1877. It led to the roof, but without any outlet, which suggested that the block was of earlier construction than Charles Maitland's work in 1664.

From its present position the old keep comes naturally into a description of the interior. Its south and east walls are respectively about 32 feet and 22 feet within the present south and east walls. When disentangled from the additions it is found to be of the L shape, its east line about 52 feet and its south line about 44 feet; but probably its first form was a tower of rectangular shape, with a south line of 44 feet and the east line 35 feet, to which was later added another rectangle extending the east line another 17 feet to the north, with a north line of 27 feet. This supposition is supporthe by the existence of a fine old wheel stair in the north wall of ted main block, where the added wall of the other block springs off on the west and forms what is known as the " re-entering angle." The entrance to the old castle was therefore probably near the centre of the north wall, the whole L-shaped building forming a typical Scottish house, with walls of a uniform thickness of about 10 feet.

On the ground floor is a vaulted room, and above that a similar room. That on the first floor is entered from the wheel stair by an angled passage. The floor space is 12 feet by 11, and the height to the centre of the arched roof 7 feet. There is a finely splayed window with stone seats and a narrow opening. The two rooms are thought to have been guard-rooms.

The principal rooms of the present day are all in the later parts

HATTON HOUSE
THE WEST AND SOUTH FRONTS

HATTON HOUSE
THE ENTRANCE HALL

surrounding the old fortalice. The main hall, entered from the east through a smaller hall, is a charming room of dimensions 50 feet by 20. At the south-west corner a doorway leads into a narrow passage which runs east to west along the south line of the keep; and from this passage the library and morning-room are reached. The morning-room stands between the library and dining-room, and the latter room has an extension into the round tower of the south-west angle—this recess being kept as a separate room because it was Lord Jeffrey's working room when he was tenant of the house.

On the first floor two rooms, the saloon and the drawing-room, correspond in position and dimension with the hall and the library. In the days when Maitland did his work Memel pine was greatly used in Scottish houses; and this house was one of them. But it was long unoccupied and much of the wood decayed, so the present owner has replaced it, often with wood panelling from other old houses.

The entrance-hall is panelled in oak brought from Litheringham Abbey, Suffolk. The walls of the dining-room are panelled in oak in its natural colour and state. The morning-room has the only original oak in the house. It was covered with several coats of paint according to the evil practice of the past; but this has had the advantage of maturing and beautifying it for the present generation.

Lord Jeffrey's study in the tower is very small but very interesting. As in the house at Craigcrook, the judge chose the smallest room in the house. This room is nine-sided and very decorative, and it looks as if the colours, though appearing fresh, are those of Jeffrey's time, blue with gold lines and a gold cornice. The centre of the ceiling is a painting of a man flying away with a lightly clothed female who does not seem to mind either the abduction or the chilliness of the aerial regions—a deeply classical subject. The interior, taking all the rooms, is a delightful testimony to the artistic sense of the present laird and to the possibility of adding modern grace to ancient design without detriment to either.

The early name of the house and estate was Halton, and the first laird whose name is known was John de Halton, to whom Robert II. granted a confirmation of the town and lands of Haltoun, dated and sealed at Scone, June 11, 1374. In 1377 he sold the estate to Allan de Lawdre " for a certain sum of money paid by the said Allan to him for aliment of his body, in his great necessity "— as quoted in a private work by the late Sir John R. Findlay entitled *Hatton House* and printed in 1875.

The purchase by Lauder introduces a long chapter of history, for the Lauders retained possession from 1377 until 1652, when

Richard Lauder of Hatton settled the property on his daughter Elizabeth on her marriage with Charles Maitland. The Earls of Lauderdale remained owners until the 8th Earl sold Hatton to Miss Scott of Scotstarvet, who became Duchess of Portland.

Her trustees sold the estate in 1797 to James Gibson of Ingleston, afterwards Sir James Gibson-Craig, Baronet, of Riccarton. He broke up the estate into lots, of which that including the house was bought by the Reverend Thomas Randall, who afterwards took the name of Davidson. The present Archbishop of Canterbury belongs to that family.

Thomas Davidson sold Hatton to the Earl of Morton in 1870 ; the Earl transferred it to his son Lord Aberdour ; and Lord Aberdour sold it to James McKelvie in 1898. The next sale was to the present owner in 1915. In the days when Lord Jeffrey occupied it as tenant, Francis Horner, Lord Cockburn, and the other celebrities of Edinburgh society, social and literary, often met there.

XXVI

HAWTHORNDEN, LASSWADE, MIDLOTHIAN

"DRUMMOND of Hawthornden," the Scottish poet of the end of the sixteenth century and the beginning of the seventeenth, made his beloved home of Hawthornden immortal; but it deserves that gift on account of its own beauty. The present owner is a lineal descendant of the poet's father, Sir John Drummond, first of Hawthornden, and is Sir James Hamlyn Williams Williams-Drummond, 5th Baronet, who lives on his Welsh estate of Edwinsford, Llandilo, inherited through the marriage of his grandfather, Sir James Drummond, the 3rd Baronet, with Mary Eleanor, second daughter and co-heiress of Sir James Hamlyn Williams, 3rd Baronet, of Clovelly Court and Edwinsford.

The River North Esk flows through the grounds, forming the "den," and Sir Walter Scott wrote of the locality in *The Lay of the Last Minstrel*—

> " O'er Roslin all that dreary night
> A wondrous blaze was seen to gleam ;
> 'Twas broader than the watch-fire light,
> And redder than the bright moonbeam.
>
> " It glared on Roslin's castled rock,
> It ruddied all the copse-wood glen ;
> 'Twas seen from Dryden's groves of oak,
> And seen from cavern'd Hawthornden."

The Den is wonderfully deep and close, with great rugged perpendicular rocks rising threateningly from the bed of the stream. On an almost insulated rock rose that first fortress of historical times of which we have definite knowledge. It was held by a branch of the family of Abernethy, of whose origin little is known but something conjectured—that the representative of the family in the twelfth century held the office of Lay Abbot of the Culdee Abbey of Abernethy in Strathearn.

When the War of Independence followed the aggression of Edward I. of England, the castle of Hawthornden was held by Sir Lawrence de Abernethy, son of Sir William de Abernethy of Saltoun.

He was a persistent adherent of the English interest and was on his way to help Edward II. when he met the Douglas in hot pursuit of the English after Bannockburn ; so he changed sides at once and joined in the pursuit. But he was on the wrong side again in 1337, and the result was some confusion in the possession of the estate, from which the Abernethys ultimately emerged still as possessors of Hawthornden. They passed the property on to the Douglas family through a female ; and the Douglas family sold it to Sir John Drummond, son of Sir Robert Drummond, Master of Works to King James V.

The general aspect of the castle and its surroundings can best be realised from a hillock not far from the buildings, slightly to the east, with a hollow between the hillock and the house. The old " keep " stands up majestically, with a later house built on to it at the west. The old stronghold is not later than the fifteenth century, and parts of the walls may go back to any remote age, while the foundations are doubtless hundreds of years older than the visible masonry. The " keep " is 27 feet by 23—the usual dimensions of an early building of that type.

The later house has an inscription on the east wall—" Divino munere Gulielmus Drummondus Johannis equitis aurati filius ut honesto otio quiesceret sibi et successoribus instauravit anno 1638," all in capital letters : " By the Divine gift William Drummond, son of the gilded knight John, in order that he might live in honourable ease, restored me for himself and his successors in the year 1638."

Part of the interest of the inscription lies in the fact that it is the poet's. Further interest lies in the question of the date of the building of the house, for it is practically certain that the castle was destroyed in the English invasions of 1544 and 1547. Was the house built by the Douglases thereafter, or was it built by the poet's father, or by the poet himself? A tablet containing the Scott arms over a dormer window is attributed to Sir John's day ; but the Scott arms only came with the marriage of the poet's son Sir William to Barbara, daughter of Sir William Scott of Clerkington.

Besides the old castle and the house adjoining it there are extensive remains of strong buildings to the north of the " keep," across an avenue which runs north and south. Part of these buildings formed a guard-house to the castle and stands high above it, and Queen Mary is said to have slept three nights there ; but there is no tradition of the date. Interesting relics of the Queen which the owner possesses may belong to that time. They are a pair of evening slippers with very high heels, and a dress of brocade, richly embroidered in blue, green, yellow, and gold—well preserved and still beautiful.

HAWTHORNDEN
THE NORTH FRONT, AND "THE LOVERS' LOUP"

HAWTHORNDEN
THE OLD KEEP

The slippers are of a rich cream colour, of fine leather, figured in colours corresponding with the dress. James Grant, in *Old and New Edinburgh*, attributes the relics to Annabella Drummond, wife of King Robert III., but the family knows of no such tradition.

On a window of the old guard-house are the initials and date " W.D. 1716," evidently those of the poet's great-grandson. The old castle buildings which extended west from the "keep" are now represented by a ruined wall which forms the southern boundary of the small courtyard. It was part of the great banqueting-hall, still impressive by the thickness of the walls and its massive grandeur. In its perfect state it must have been an imposing pile ; and probably Hertford left it much as it is now when he destroyed the castle in 1544 in the warlike wooing of a little lass.

The north front presents a wonderful view, as it is built on the edge of a cliff overlooking a tremendous chasm, the ravine in which the river flows. Near it is a rock known as " The Lovers' Loup " from a tradition that two lovers sprang from it rather than face separation. This front is the back of the house as distinguished from the old castle. It has the Scottish features of a round tower, two dormer windows, and two crow-stepped gables.

The entrance to the courtyard is close to the keep and is in a very thick wall with horizontal shot-holes. On the door is a knocker which tradition says belonged to King Robert III., and above are the arms of Drummond and Scott.

Among the Hawthornden relics is a two-handed sword which belonged to King Robert Bruce. It is 5 feet 2 inches in length and has a quadruple guard of cross shape 11 inches from point to point. These are my measurements. The blade is practically straight, much worn and not very thick, a business-like weapon. Another relic is a table which belonged to King Robert III. and his wife Annabella Drummond. The front parts are handsomely carved and the back parts strengthened by plain legs. A centre panel on the front has the lion rampant of Scotland and the date 1396, while at the corners are repeated the initials " R.S." in monogram, with " III " beneath. In the centre of the ends is the monogram " AD." An ivory walking-stick is also interesting. It is said to have belonged to the famous Duchess of Lauderdale, but it certainly did belong a century later to Bishop Abernethy-Drummond, a representative of the first owners of Hawthornden; he married Barbara Drummond, great-great-grand-daughter of the poet, and heiress of Hawthornden, thus uniting the two lines of Abernethy and Drummond. By another line the present laird represents both of these families.

Among the many paintings is one of the poet, dated 1694, and possibly by Mytens. Raeburn is represented by Captain Sir John Forbes-Drummond, R.N., the first baronet, and by Lady Drummond, wife of the second baronet.

A most extraordinary feature of the castle is the series of caves in the rocks adjoining the house. Tradition says that one of the caves is really that in which Robert Bruce watched the spider, although the story associates the island of Rathlin with the incident.

There is a famous sycamore near the house, one of " the four sisters," and it is said that Drummond the poet was sitting under it when Ben Jonson arrived after his long walk from London in 1618. The visit is known to have bored Drummond badly.

XXVII

HOPETOUN HOUSE, WEST LOTHIAN

HOPETOUN HOUSE, the seat of the Marquis of Linlithgow, is situated in the parish of Abercorn, in the county of Linlithgow, and not far from South Queensferry. The estate lies on a beautiful terrace which overlooks the Firth of Forth. On the opposite side is the old and famous Rosyth Castle, still in existence, but surrounded by the great harbour works which were so important an element in our defence during the Great War, although they were not quite ready when the War began.

The estate has been formed out of a considerable number of former separate estates. Philipstoun, Stoneyhill, and Morton, formerly belonged to branches of the Dundas family; Duntarvie belonged to the Durhams, a family which at one time owned a large amount of land; Midhope was the property of the Earls of Linlithgow, whose title was attainted and has not been restored; Craigton was a possession of the Ewings; and Duddingstoun belonged to Gabriel Hamilton Dundas.

The house is one of the most palatial in Scotland, and is reached from Edinburgh by the great Queensferry Road and a road which branches off to the left about a mile from South Queensferry. A great avenue through a wide and practically open expanse leads straight up to the house, in front of which stretches a lawn of magnificent extent, round part of which at the sides a kind of fosse marks the raising of the lawn to a level. The central avenue through the lawn is very striking on account of its width. A drive extends on each side of the lawn from the central avenue, swinging round at right angles when it reaches the wings of the house, and then moving inward on either side to a great gravel space which forms a kind of forecourt.

At the back of the house is another extensive lawn, flanked by trees, and having at its open part towards the west an artificial lake. Probably the gardens cannot be excelled in Scotland.

The main front of the house faces practically due east, and with its centre block and great wings extending in front forms a great curve enclosing the forecourt. It was not all built as a single effort; nor was it even planned as a whole in its present form, although it is so harmonious in all its details that it seems to have been built to one design. The main buildings in the centre were begun by the first Earl of Hopetoun in 1696, and Sir William Bruce of Kinross was his architect. That part of the work appears to have been completed in 1702. The centre part is a great block of something over 100 feet in line. The symmetry of the building seems to show that the first design, completed in 1702, included north and south wings on the east front; and these wings are each about 100 feet in width from north to south, making the total length of the house as finished by Sir William Bruce about 300 feet. Probably Sir William, with his expansive ideas, looked forward to completing Hopetoun House on something like its present lines; but that was left to Robert Adam, the pupil and son of Sir William's pupil William Adam.

His additions are found in the north and south wings, and in the colonnades which join them to Sir William Bruce's work—a vast enlargement, making a building of impressive extent. The wings stand out over 200 feet from the original line of the east front, and each presents to the east a front line of about 120 feet wide. From the south wall of the south wing to the north wall of the north wing I make by a rough measurement to be about 520 feet; and that is the length of frontage which an approach presents to the eye, the opening of the forecourt being about 300 feet wide.

The general character of the masonry is " ashlar "—smoothly dressed stone in regular courses over 12 inches deep; while in the lowest storey of the main building the edges of the courses are slightly bevelled or splayed, leaving a little space between them— which is known as " rustic." The centre block is approached by a great flight of fifteen broad stone steps, without balustrade or parapet, leading to a spacious stone platform from which the house is entered. From end to end fifteen fluted pilasters with Corinthian capitals divide the second and third storeys into bays and carry a narrow frieze and cornice the whole way.

The colonnades spring away on each side from the wings in a concave curve. There are ten columns in each colonnade, standing on plain low bases, all the columns smooth and rounded, Doric in simplicity, and with only a square flat slab for capital. The arcade or cloister enclosed is just wide enough to form a passage. Then comes Adam's square wing, highly classical in character. All the details of the back of the house are in the classical style, ever varying, and showing a great deal of the same architectural feeling which marks Kinross House, which Sir William Bruce built as his own home.

The interior is in full keeping with the magnificent exterior, both in its style and its contents. The great flight of steps on the

HOPETOUN HOUSE
THE NORTH END
OF THE EAST FRONT

HOPETOUN HOUSE
THE HALL

east front leads to the entrance on the first floor. This admits to the outer hall, from which, passing straight on, we enter the inner hall; and from the inner hall the main staircase leads to the upper floors. Still advancing, we enter the garden room, which is the ordinary dining-room and looks out from the west front. Returning to the inner hall, the library is entered on the north side of the great central square block.

The outer hall has a semi-domed or "coved" roof, is almost square, and is completely oak panelled. The inner hall is octagonal in form and open to the roof, with a dome light. It is panelled in oak and the dome is adorned with paintings in the style of frescoes. Most of the paintings in this hall and on the staircase are fitted into panels and are in the classical style.

The saloon is a delightful room entered from the outer hall on the right. It departs from the oak-panelling scheme which is found in other rooms, and has many decorative features. But its great glory is its examples of the great masters of painting—"The Adoration of the Shepherds," by Rubens; "The Emperor Charles V.," by Titian; "The Marquis di Spinola," by Vandyke; "Ecce Homo," by Vandyke; "Titian," by Tintoretto; "The Mother of Rembrandt," by Rembrandt; "A Lady at Ablutions," by Paul Veronese; and a characteristic small painting by Antonio Canaletto, the great architectural painter of Venice in the eighteenth century.

The red drawing-room comes next, about 60 feet long, with a very handsome coved ceiling. It is a very decorative room with many charming features, furnished in the French manner, with much gilding, the gold note appearing in the decorative ceiling. In spite of its own features, the glory of this room lies in its paintings, "St. Francis," by Guido Reni; "Isabella, Governess of the Netherlands," by Vandyke; "A Lady," by Cornelius Janssen; "Christ and the Woman at the Well," by Francesco Barbieri, commonly known as Il Guercino (the squint-eyed); "St. John and the Lamb," by Andrea Proccacini; "Three Heads and a Dog," by Anibale Caracci; "Cattle," by Benjamin Cuyp; and a very large number of others by the "Old Masters."

The great dining-room occupies the end of the north wing of the Bruce house, and it has a fine outlook on the Firth of Forth. Scottish painters are well represented in it—Aikman by "Charles, 1st Earl of Hopetoun," in armour; Watson Gordon by "Lord Macdonald" and the 4th and 5th Earls; Allan Ramsay by the 2nd Earl; Jamesone, the "Scottish Vandyke," by Sir Thomas Hope, the King's Advocate of the reign of Charles I. This last is very like that by Jamesone in Pinkie House.

The library, to the right of the centre hall as we look west, has above the fireplace a painting by Raeburn of the Lord President Hope, and has also many specimens of illuminated manuscripts of very ancient date, besides some examples of early printing. This description may perhaps give some conception of the splendour of Hopetoun House; but it would take a long chapter to give an adequate idea.

The history of the family is very interesting. The founder of it came from France in the train of Magdalene, the French princess who was the first wife of King James V. She came to Scotland in 1537; and that is the year in which John de Hope began to be a Scotsman. He had a son Edward, who was a Commissioner to the Scots Parliament of 1560. Edward had a son Thomas, who was followed by a son of the same Christian name who became the King's Advocate—that is, according to the modern term, the Lord Advocate —and died in 1646. He had six sons, of whom three were judges while he was Lord Advocate. The eldest was Lord Craighall, and the sixth was Sir James Hope of Hopetoun, the founder of the Hopetoun branch, who became a Lord of Session with the judicial title of Lord Hopetoun. He was succeeded by his eldest son John in 1661, and John was drowned in the wreck of H.M. Frigate *Gloucester*, which was bringing the Duke of York to Scotland in 1682. It was in the long minority of John's son Charles, born in 1681, that Hopetoun House was built, and Charles became the 1st Earl in 1703. Besides distinction in Law, there has also been distinction in War, and the 4th Earl is famous as Sir John Moore's Lieutenant. And so went on the line to the present Hope of Hopetoun, who is the 8th Earl of Hopetoun and the 2nd Marquis of Linlithgow.

XXVIII

KINROSS HOUSE, TOWN AND COUNTY OF KINROSS

THE same architect who planned the central part of Hopetoun House planned and built Kinross House as his own home. He was Sir William Bruce of Kinross, the second son of Robert Bruce, the 3rd Baron of Blairhill in Perthshire. I cannot find a reliable date for his birth, but it must have been in the later years of the reign of James VI. Towards the end of the Cromwell despotism he was beginning to take some part in politics, and it is said that he was a channel of communication between the exiled King Charles II. and General Monk, even conveying to Charles that General's offer of service. He held office under the King from the Restoration, and in 1668 had progressed so far as to acquire the lands of Balcaskie and to be made a baronet. In 1671 he was King's Surveyor and Master of Works, and in that office designed the restoration and rebuilding of Holyrood Palace. In 1675 he bought the estate of Kinross, with Loch Leven, from the Earl of Morton, and from that time he was " Bruce of Kinross."

He is described by an authority on Scottish architecture as being rather an amateur than a professional architect, but very successful. Holyrood Palace gave him an outlet for a natural taste, and he proceeded to express himself further in the same direction. It is through his disciple and apprentice William Adam that he has been an abiding influence on Scottish architecture. William Adam's sons, Robert and James, followed their father's lines ; and a visit to Italy developed still further their Scottish adaptation of the classical style. But to Sir William Bruce belongs all the honour of the complete change from the Scottish baronial to the Scottish classical. He died in 1710, over eighty years of age.

The baronetcy became extinct after the third holder, and the estate passed by succession to James Carstairs, Sir William's grandson, who took the name of Bruce. He died in 1768, and his son James sold the estate in 1777 to George Graham, belonging to a branch of the Montrose family. George Graham had a son Thomas, whose heir was killed on board a ship which had been attacked by a privateer. So his father willed the estate to that one of his two daughters who should first have a son to reach the age of twenty-one years.   This stimulated the ladies to haste and they both married within six months of the old man's death.   One of them never had a son ; the other, who married Sir James Montgomery of Stanhope, had a son who succeeded as Sir Graham Montgomery, 3rd Baronet of Stanhope.   He never occupied Kinross House, the furniture and contents of which had been sold; and the house remained empty many years.   Nor did his son James Gordon Henry, the 4th Baronet, occupy it.   So it has been left to the present owner, Sir Basil Templar Graham-Montgomery, 5th Baronet of Stanhope in the County of Peebles, to bring both house and grounds into a condition which would delight the heart of the first owner and builder if he could see them ; and this has been accomplished since the year 1903.

When Sir William Bruce bought the property there was an old house upon it with the same name ; but only the foundations now remain, mostly buried, to the north-east of the present house.   It was in 1685 that Sir William began to build Kinross House, which is in design a rectangle, placed in a commanding situation in the centre of the gardens and grounds.   The town of Kinross seems to have grown towards the mansion, and "Avenue Road" leads right up to the lodge gate.   A wall encloses a park which is practically square.

For practical purposes the house may be said to extend from north to south, it is so little out of that line.   The main front faces west, towards the town, and is roughly 120 feet long, while the ends are about 66 feet wide.   From the ends of the west front, in which there are reminders of the fronts of Hopetoun House, walls of one storey in height curve outward, each with its open balustrade of Italian form, and ending in a pavilion with an ogee roof.   Near each pavilion is an interrupting column on which is a sphere flattened to make four sides for four sundials, of which two are recorded as made by John Hamilton, mason.

The feature which attracts first notice in the west front is the fine flight of nine steps leading to the entrance—wide at the bottom and narrowing at the top, without a balustrade, as at Hopetoun. There is a wide portico in the classical style with round pilasters and columns supporting a plain architrave with frieze and cornice, above which is a pediment.   The front consists of three sections forming a symmetrical whole of centre block and wings, the lowest storey, partly sunk, having rustic masonry and the other three storeys ashlar.   The top storey of short windows has a corbel-course under it, and a coat of arms is above the centre window of the third storey, which is above the porch.   A curious triangular marking in the wall here suggests that there was a tall pediment right up to the coat of

KINROSS HOUSE
THE WEST FRONT

KINROSS HOUSE
THE SOUTH END
OF THE BALL-ROOM

arms, occupying the space of the present window; but the same marking is to be seen in a drawing done by Sir William Bruce, so it is not later than the building of the house.

The east front and the ends carry out the impression of the west front, but on the east the basement ceases to be below the ground level. This is the garden side, and the side which takes us to the shores of Loch Leven, by a magnificent grass avenue which takes off from a flight of handsome steps at the terrace, and leads on to the "Fish Gate" near the shore. From the portico on the east front there is a very impressive view of the gardens. Below is the terrace, with closely cut hedges trained to resemble walls. In the terrace, close to the south end of the house, is a great crouching lion in white stone on a pedestal. Trees and shrubs dot the terrace, many trained into various forms among which the spiral is conspicuous. A central feature is a fountain, with flower beds arranged around it. The fountain statuary represents a naked classical figure engaged in a struggle with a swan, from the uplifted bill of which springs the column of water.

The "Fish Gate" opens upon the rough grassy ground between the surrounding wall and the loch. There is a fine view of the island, with its castle rising clearly. There can be no doubt that the thoughts of the builder of the house went out to the memory of the imprisoned Queen when he designed the arrangement which brings the castle into so prominent a view.

The interior of the house is reached by a magificent hall, about 70 feet in length, which occupies the centre part of the west front. To the north opens a small hall, and from it ascends the grand staircase. To the south of the great hall is the library, occupying the south-west corner of the building. Behind the great entrance-hall the drawing-room, divided into two parts, occupies a similar space in the east front. The south section of the drawing-room is known as "the oak drawing-room." On the upper floor are many fine rooms, one of which calls for special notice and is the ball-room, situated above the great entrance-hall and of the same dimensions.

The oak staircase which springs from the small hall is the original staircase built by Sir William Bruce. A fresco along the stairway was also done in his time. The carving of the stair balustrade is really remarkable; and it is said that the carving and the ceiling were done by a Dutch artist and his wife who travelled Scotland doing such work.

The main drawing-room has a beautiful piece of Flemish tapestry, representing a subject which seems to have been popular with the old weavers, as Mr. Graham Montgomery, son of Sir Basil, was surprised to see the same picture on an old tapestry in one of his tours in France.

The ball-room is splendid in its proportions. Its beautiful ceiling is a partial dome—that is, it is coved. It is a copy of the old ceiling above the grand staircase, the copy being by Sir Basil Montgomery, the Laird, and the original by the builder. On the north wall hangs a painting by Hoppner of the first wife of Sir James Montgomery; and on the opposite wall is one by Sir Henry Raeburn, of great beauty, representing Miss Graham of Kinross, who carried the estate into the Montgomery family, and was the grandmother of the present laird.

The name Kinross carries us back to the days of Celtic or Pictish domination. It is made up of the two common Gaelic words *ceann*, a *head*, and *ross*, a *peninsula*—as in Kinloch, the head of the loch, and the Ross of Mull, the great peninsula which fronts Iona. So that Kinross means the head of the peninsula—no doubt the spike of land jutting into Loch Leven.

Probably the history in short of the house with that name is something like this—a primitive dwelling on piles on the spit of land ; a stone fort on the island added ; the stone fort strengthened by Comgall, King of the Picts, at the end of the fifth century ; Comgall's fort replaced by the feudal castle ; the feudal castle disused for the more convenient and less isolated old Kinross House ; and last of all the present beautiful residence.

XXIX

LAMINGTON HOUSE, LANARKSHIRE

LAMINGTON HOUSE is the Lanarkshire seat of Charles Wallace Alexander Napier Cochrane-Baillie, G.C.M.G., G.C.I.E., the second Baron Lamington. It lies in a most picturesque and charming country almost on the bank of the River Clyde. Two peaks rise on opposite sides of the river, not far distant from Lamington House. They are Tinto Hill and Culter Fell, of which Tinto is 2,335 feet high and Culter 2,454; and the local rhyme has it that there are

> " Between Tintock Tap and Coulter Fell
> But scarce three handbreadths and an ell."

Lamington railway station stands 700 feet above sea-level, and Lamington House is much about the same.

At the present day the surroundings are wonderfully beautiful, especially if the district is visited when the sun is shining brilliantly, as I have seen it, on the broad valley, the undulating hills, the extensive fields of ripening grain, and the pretty village. But the district was not always like that. From various circumstances there was at one time great uncertainty as to who would be the ultimate owner; and the result was general stagnation. Mrs. Ware Scott, a connection of the family, printed in 1878 for private circulation a very striking description of the conditions which prevailed when Mr. Cochrane-Baillie, father of the present Lord Lamington, succeeded in 1836. The account is entitled *Lamington : Past and Present.*

Everything was rougher than the imagination can now picture, and the whole place neglected, a state of matters which must have had a very long existence, for Burns described a visit which he had paid to the neighbourhood. He attended service in Lamington church, and wrote—

> " A cauld, cauld day December blew,
> A cauld, cauld kirk and in't but few,
> A caulder minister never spak'—
> They'll a' be warm ere I come back."

Mrs. Ware Scott describes the young laird's arrival in a carriage—a thing which the people had never seen, and which gave them unbounded astonishment. "Still," she writes, "it was the old place. It was the home of the Chief of the Baillies." There was no house for him, and he decided to build a shooting-lodge on the site then occupied by the Inn. It was only to be two or three rooms ; but that was the beginning of Lamington House. Whether any part of the walls of the old Inn remains is a moot point, all the more difficult to solve because the house has grown sideways and endways, so that now it is not even known on what part of the present site the old Inn stood. There may be portions of the lower parts of the old walls concealed in the new.

There is an almost confusing variety of outline in the ground plan, but the house may be described generally as an oblong with the greater length from north to south, the total length of the rectangle about 90 feet and the width about 50. On all the fronts it is mainly a two-storeyed house, with gables which form a third storey. The part which strikes the eye first on approaching is the entrance, with the large double-mullioned window to the right of it. The two form a part which projects, with a pediment or gablet above each, the near ends meeting. Above the entrance is a panel with the date 1883 surmounted by a coronet and accompanied by a monogram in which the significant initial is that indicating Alexander, the Christian name of the builder. Under the date is a Latin inscription in three lines of capitals—" Pax intrantibus, Salus exeuntibus, Benedictio habitantibus "—Peace to those coming in, safety to those going out, a blessing to those dwelling within. Over the window is the coat of arms of the family, with its supporters, two lions rampant, and the coronet of a baron above.

The west front presents a great diversity of detail; it has half a dozen gables and gablets, almost all the windows on the ground floor are mullioned and transomed, dormers are placed far back, and curious angular windows are interspersed along the front, while the interest of this view is enhanced by the arrangement of hedges and the rise of the ground to the north-west. The other fronts have the same architectural features. The immediate surroundings are very pretty, and one of the most charming bits is near the south-west angle, where a sequestered nook surrounded by hedges is known as the " Persian Garden." Trees overhang it, but its most enchanting feature is its swimming pond, into which is led the Lamington Burn, or part of it.

A little journey up the hill to the north-west takes us to a very pretty chapel built by the late Alexander Baillie-Cochrane, M.P., and consecrated on August 10, 1857. Over the porch on the north side is a curious stone cross which was brought from the Appian Way at Rome, literally picked up on the road by Mrs. Baillie-Cochrane, as she was then.

The same notes which characterise the exterior architecture are found in the interior—lightness, brightness, and variety ; and these notes harmonise perfectly with the clear air and the sunshine of a locality which belongs to the uplands of Lanarkshire. The small porch admits to an open outer hall which is divided into two parts open to each other. One part is directly in front of us and the other to the right. The walls in both are of a dark green colour and are wood-lined half-way up. That on the right is a summer dining-room, very charming, and both divisions have a parquet floor.

At the back of the main part of the outer hall four steps lead downward to " the Wallace hall "; and of all the delightful rooms in the house this is in many respects the most fascinating, shaped like a capital **L**. The western arm leads to a long corridor which traverses the house from north to south and gives entrance to several rooms. The other arm, the southern, leads to the conservatory, so built as to form a continuation of the room.

To the left of the outer hall is a writing-room by the side of the conservatory. The other reception rooms are all on the west side of the long corridor, in line with each other and lighted from the west. The drawing-room is at the south end of that line ; and north of that room is a very long room of a ceremonial character, long as compared with its width. The line of rooms is terminated on the north by the dining-room, which contains three paintings of special interest. One of them is of the first Lord Lamington, the builder of the house, and is after Le Bœuf. Another is that of Admiral Sir Alexander Cochrane, G.C.B., by Sir Thomas Lawrence. The third is of George III., and is after Sir Joshua Reynolds.

Although the house is modern, there is still left standing a bit of the old castle about a mile to the north-west and close to the River Clyde. There would be more of it left but for the zeal of a factor who had it blown up in 1780 so that he might use the stones for the building of dykes. The proprietor, who was the wife of Sir John Lockhart Ross of Balnagown, tried to stop it when she heard, but she was only in time to save the north-west angle, the greater part of the west wall, and part of the north wall. Its name, " Wallace's Tower," connects it with the great patriot, to whom tradition says that it belonged. And tradition also connects the present family with Sir William Wallace.

Blind Harry's metrical history is responsible for most of what has been recorded of Wallace, but Andrew Wyntoun's *Orygynale Cronykil of Scotland* is more trustworthy.

Tradition says that Wallace's wife was Marion Braidfute, whose father was Hugh de Braidfute, owner of Lamington. Further, that they had a daughter, who was taken to Lamington for safety, and that she married Sir William Baillie, and that thus Lamington became a possession of the Baillies. Other accounts say that this is true so far as the marriage is concerned, but that Lamington was at that time a Seton possession, and became a Baillie property by a daughter of the Setons marrying a son of Sir William Baillie and of Wallace's daughter. His name also was William, and he rests on historical evidence, as he obtained a charter in 1367 from King David II. of " the whole barony of Lambiston." From his time the descent of the Baillies is clear, and the family provided many historical and eminent personages. But the last seven generations inherit the name of Baillie in the female line, with Carmichael, Dundas, Lockhart, Ross, and Cochrane on the male side. The old name of Baillie, derived like Balliol from the Flemish town of Bailleul, and associated so romantically with that of Wallace, has lost nothing by the alliances, while it has retained its distinctive individuality.

LAMINGTON HOUSE
THE SOUTH FRONT

LAMINGTON HOUSE
THE LIBRARY

XXX

LENNOXLOVE, HADDINGTON, EAST LOTHIAN

THE name Lennoxlove has a romantic sound which seems to carry us back to the days of knightly deeds. Its history bears out the suggestion of the sound, and there is romance about the way in which the name was acquired. It is the old Lethington Tower, a possession of the Maitlands of Lethington from the time when they bought it from the Giffords of Yester in the fourteenth century. In the days of Charles II. the Maitland who owned it was the Duke of Lauderdale. The county lairds of East Lothian in those days had their town houses in Haddington, and used to dine together periodically. The story goes that Lord Blantyre, who had no land in the county, often used to join the lairds, and that the Duke resented this. His peculiar way of showing his feeling was by offering to sell Lethington to Blantyre, who he knew was too poor to buy it. He made the offer so frequently that Blantyre got tired of the joke.

Lord Blantyre had a beautiful cousin, Frances Teresa Stuart, who had married the Duke of Lennox and Richmond, and was one of the reigning beauties of the Court—said to be the original of the effigy of " Britannia " on our coins. She advised Blantyre to accept the offer the next time it should be made ; and he did so. The Duchess of Lennox sent her cousin the purchase money in a casket which is still preserved at Lennoxlove—" with the Duchess of Lennox's love." Lethington became the property of Lord Blantyre, who changed the name to Lennoxlove ; and Lennoxlove is still in the hands of a descendant of that Lord Blantyre.

The casket is a silver-gilt toilet service of exquisite workmanship, in a case or casket, the whole having been a gift from King Charles II. to the beautiful Duchess.

The house is about a mile and a half to the south of Haddington, in the direction of Gifford and the Lammermuir Hills. The Gifford Water flows through the grounds and has some excellent trout pools. The woods are usually said to have been planted by the only Duke of Lauderdale ; but in reality the particularly fine specimens of oak

117

and beech were mostly planted between 1776 and 1812 by the
10th and 11th Lords Blantyre.

A curious tale attaches to the wall surrounding the demesne.
It is said that James, Duke of York, who came to Scotland in 1680,
had remarked disparagingly to the Duke of Lauderdale that he
understood that there was not a single walled park in Scotland. The
Duke set himself to prove the contrary, got his people to work, and
in a very short time had his grounds ready for show with a 12-feet
high wall round them. The north wall still stands, with its original
arch, though not its original gate ; and the other walls are there
without their gateways. Lethington appears to have been the first
residential park in Scotland with an enclosing wall.

The old tower remains the centre of interest, forming the west
part of the present south front of the extended house. At the east
end of the line is a second tower of practically the same height,
believed to be a Maitland addition of the date 1644, as the south-east
corner wall bears a sundial with that date, beside the balcony of a
small room adjoining the drawing-room. That tower had formerly
a crow-stepped gable, which disappeared when the tower was raised
in height about 1810.

The old tower can hardly be dated later than the year 1400.
In the middle of the fourteenth century Sir Robert Maitland of
Thirlestane obtained a charter of the lands of Lethington, and there
was probably a strong house on the estate then. As we see the old
tower now, it presents the familiar Scottish L shape, with a south
and a west face and an entrance in the angle. The old entrance is
now in the interior, but distinct, with its Latin inscription : " Quis-
nam e Maetellana stirpe fundamenta jecerit, quis turrim excitav-
erit in vida celavit antiquitas, luminaria auxit, faciliorem ascensum
praebuit, ornationem reddidit Joannes Maetellanus Lauderiae comes
an aere Chr. MDCXXVI." The meaning is : " Whoever of the
Maitland family laid the foundations, whoever raised the tower on a
vacant spot, time has concealed. But John Maitland, Earl of
Lauderdale, has increased the windows, provided an easier stair,
and added adornment in the year 1626 of the Christian era."
Buildings still later than 1626 almost cover the top.

On the first floor is a very fine room, the original great hall,
with a length from north to south of 39 feet and a width of 21 feet.
It has a fine vaulted roof and a grand old fireplace, while its walls
are 10 feet thick. The fireplace has been restored by the present
Laird and has a carved coat of arms above it with his and his
wife's initials—" W.A.B." and " H.C.E.C." This fine room was
long used as a kitchen, but now its head has been raised again to

LENNOXLOVE
THE SOUTH FRONT

LENNOXLOVE
THE ENTRANCE HALL

due honour as a baronial hall. From the old entrance it can be approached by the old wheel stair in the angle, still guarded by the old iron " Yett."

The first famous Maitland of Lethington, Sir Richard, a Lord of Session and the 12th laird, who became blind, praised his house in verse—

> " Greit wes the wark to houke the grounde,
> And thy foundation cast ;
> But greiter it wes than to found,
> And end thee at the last.
> I marvel that he did not feir,
> Wha raisit thee on hicht,
> That no foundation should thee beir,
> But thou should sink for wecht."

The rest of the south front is about equal in length to the tower. On the east side is an old-fashioned garden with paved walks, very old, but arranged about twenty years ago as an old Dutch garden. The main entrance to the house is not in the old tower but about the middle of that front, and admits to a hall of extremely elegant design, with a ceiling supported by a wide flattened arch to the left, and a similar arch in front, by which the great staircase is approached. There is a fine portrait by Raeburn of Sir David Baird, who led the storming party at Seringapatam in 1799 and lost an arm at Corunna. When he was a prisoner of Hyder Ali, and it was reported to his mother that he had been sent up country chained to another prisoner, her comment is said to have been : " De'il help the chiel that's chained to oor Davie." The present laird is his great-grand-nephew.

On the right of the hall is the library, an oak-panelled room with ceiling and fireplace copied from the old tower, and above the fireplace the Lethington arms and the date 1619. The old rooms have many indications of their age, but they are sufficiently modernised for comfort.

A more prosaic account of the Blantyre acquisition is that the Duchess of Lennox, who died in 1702, left the bulk of her property to her cousin's son Walter, afterwards 6th Lord Blantyre, for the purchase of estates which were to be called after her. Lethington was bought from Lord Teviot, who had bought it from the 4th Earl of Lauderdale, nephew of the Duke. The Blantyre family retained Lennoxlove until the death of the 12th lord, when the male line ceased—extinct or dormant. The second daughter of Lord Blantyre had married Sir David Baird, Baronet, of Newbyth ; and their second son, William Arthur, inherited Lennoxlove. In 1908 he married the Lady Hersey Constance Evelyn Conyngham, third daughter of the 4th Marquis Conyngham.

The blind poet, Sir Richard Maitland, who was born in 1496, was the father of both Secretary Maitland and Chancellor Maitland, the Lauderdale family being descended from the Chancellor. The poet's collection of manuscripts is now in the Library of Magdalene College, Cambridge ; it was bought by Samuel Pepys at the sale of the library of the Duke. It is commonly said that the collection is now worth more than its weight in gold, for without it a great deal of the early poetry of Scotland would be lost.

The old poet would have had much scope today to continue his verses on women's vanity in dress ; he thought his own day very bad :

> " Some wifis of the borowstoun
> Sae wonder vain ar, and wantoun,
> In warld they watt not quhat to weir ;
> On claithis they wair mony a croun ;
> And all for newfangleness of geir."

This was only a general indictment, and when he went into details about petticoats, or " wilicoats," he thought them ruinous. But nice " petties " encouraged them to nice hose, and to show them :

> " Sometimes they will beir up their gown,
> To shaw their wilicoat hingand down ;
> And sometimes baith they will upbeir,
> To shaw their hose of black or brown ;
> And all for newfangleness of geir."

It distressed the old man ; and the country girls—" landwart ladies " —were just as naughty as the townswomen.

XXXI

LESLIE HOUSE, LESLIE, FIFE

THE estate of Leslie is situated in three parishes, Leslie, Markinch, and Kinglassie, but the house is in the parish of the same name. There is a village of Leslie also, lying practically at the base of the two Lomond peaks, which stand up so prominently in Fife and are visible across the Firth of Forth from the Lothians. The village is only five miles distant from the famous Loch Leven. The origin of the name has more than one explanation. Fetkil was the name of the parish in a distant day, until the Earl of Rothes gave it his family name. Another account is more difficult to follow. The River Leven, which enters the sea at the town of Leven, flows past the village of Leslie, and some explain the name as compounded of two particles, *Lis*, meaning a garden, and the name of the river— so, Lisleven or Lisleen, the garden by the River Leven. This derivation has a certain amount of support from the fact that the village is on a beautiful table-land, which in past days had so many advantages that it was made by royalty the scene of games and sports. Leslie Green is said to be the scene of King James's poem *Christis Kirk on the Green*.

The first of the Leslies of this house whom we know is Malcolm, son of Bartolf, in the twelfth century. He was Constable of Inverurie Castle in Aberdeenshire ; and his great-grandson, Sir Norman Leslie, is stated to have acquired Fetkill or Fythkill, about the year 1282. George Leslie was made a Lord of Parliament in 1445 as Lord Leslie of Leven, and was afterwards created Earl of Rothes.

There are now no remains of a house previous to the year 1670, when the Duke of Rothes, the friend of Charles II., built the house on the present site. There must have been a house long before that date, but not even a tradition of it seems to survive. The house of 1670 seems to have occupied very much the same site as is now occupied. The present house has a long frontage from north to south, its entrance facing the west.

The Duke's house had at the north and south extremities wings branching east in each case. There are no such wings now, the north and south ends of the line merely projecting slightly. In spite of the fact that there is no surviving tradition of the first house, it is sometimes definitely stated that there was a house dating from the fourteenth century—a strong probability, but nothing more.

A very reliable account of the house built by the Duke of Rothes says that it was something like Holyrood Palace, built round a court and having a gallery three feet longer than that of Holyrood, one side occupied by portraits of the Rothes family, and the other by paintings of friends of the Duke. That house, which must have been very magnificent if it was ever finished in the form described, was burnt down on December 28, 1763. The present house is said by that account—the *New Statistical Account of Scotland,* published in 1845—to be only one-fourth of the size of the old house, and to have been built in 1767 by John, Earl of Rothes ; which leads us to suppose that the least damaged side was restored and the others taken down—if they had really been built.

The appearance of the west front is in keeping with this view. It is in the style of Sir William Bruce of Kinross. It is about 160 feet long, and has three storeys with a row of dormer windows above them. The whole design is symmetrical, and starts with a central part, three windows wide and three storeys high, with a broad pediment above. The doorway occupies the position of one window, and is in a plain classical style, of which the details are fluted pilasters with Doric capitals, round columns carrying a flattened arch, and a projecting keystone. The tympanum of the pediment is filled by the Rothes Arms.

To left and right of the centre part the line falls back a little, each section between centre and wing having three windows on each floor, and the storeys divided by string courses. The extremities of the line advance about four yards in front of the parts just described, and might be called wings on that account. Their details are similar to those of the other parts, but the wings are only two windows in width. A long avenue advances to this front.

The east front is the back of the house and presents a much plainer appearance. It has a terrace garden immediately in front of it, raised above the adjoining level by a few feet of a retaining wall which carries chains swung from iron supports. The paths are flagged, and the intersection of two is occupied by a fountain of classical design and considerable height. The ground immediately below the terrace extends a long way, with croquet green, tennis courts, and sports fields.

The trend of the ground is from north to south, which has led to the construction of terraces, the advantage of which can be best realised by passing down to the river. It is spanned by a bridge of decorative effect, known as " The Lady's Bridge." From here

LESLIE HOUSE
THE WEST FRONT

LESLIE HOUSE
A CORNER OF THE LOUNGE

looking north-west there is a charming view of the south end of the house rising above the terraces.

One of the main features of the interior is its fine series of tapestries. Among them is one which pictures the story of Leander. Another is the anointing of Saul to be King. There is a whole series devoted to the portrayal of the wanderings of the children of Israel in the Wilderness. The pictures are so numerous that it is impossible to give a complete list of them here.

The hall of Leslie House measures more than 30 feet each way. The ceiling is broken into squares by great beams, supported on four great round columns. Above the fireplace is a hawking scene, and on one of the walls is the tapestry of the Anointing of Saul. Opposite the entrance is a door leading to a passage which takes us through the house to the east front; while on our right is a doorway into a passage leading to the drawing-room at the south extremity of the line—the drawing-room occupying the whole width of the house. The dining-room is entered from the right of the hall and has no tapestries. The passage from the hall to the drawing-room contains a large tapestry representing mounted men repelling assailants, of whom some are in boats.

A stair starts from behind the south end of the hall and leads to the first landing, which has a long passage running north and south, opening into a lounge which is over the dining-room. Tapestries are the feature of the landing, one of them being a large sea and figure piece. One of the figures, nude, has fallen, and two females are lamenting, while Cupid stands with his bow, apparently grieved. On the north wall of the lounge is a large group tapestry. On the south is a representation of a banquet, a dish being presented and apparently provoking expressions of surprise. On the west wall women stand at a well, with pitchers, while a man and an ass stand in the middle distance—and two men appear to have surprised the women. Other rooms have tapestries also. On the top floor, occupying the space of both lounge and billiard-room, is the ball-room, of splendid dimensions, with a floor which leaves nothing to be desired. Fine tapestries are here also.

The present owner of this wonderfully attractive house, and Laird of Leslie, is Major Robert Spencer Nairn, second son of the late Sir Michael Barker Nairn, Baronet, of Rankeilour. Major Nairn held the rank of Major in the Fife and Forfar Yeomanry at the outbreak of the Great War, and served in France and at Gallipoli.

For the origin of the Leslie family we go to the old barony of the name in Aberdeenshire, the earliest possession of the family on record. Bartolf is a shadowy individual—the earliest Leslie of that Ilk. His son is clear enough. Bartolf is said to have married a sister of King Malcolm III., and to have received the lands of the Aberdeenshire Leslie for services rendered to the King. Also, he is believed to have been a Fleming, and to have died old about the year 1121. It was a descendant, Sir Norman de Leslie, who acquired Fythkill in Fife and called it Leslie. He died between 1317 and 1320, having in his time sworn allegiance to Edward I. of England and afterwards joined Robert Bruce.

There were many branches from these founders, one of them the lairds of Rothes in Elgin, and another the Leslies of Balquhain. And one whose name appears as "Andrew de Laskelyne" was a signatory to the protestation of National Independence drawn up by the Scottish barons and presented to the Pope John XXII. in 1320: the duplicate of the document is in the General Register House in Edinburgh.

The first step in the peerage came when George Leslie was made Lord Leslie of Leven in 1445, and his earldom dates from 1457. Both the barony and the earldom can go in the female line, and they have often done so. The one and only Duke was the 7th Earl, and was succeeded in the earldom by his daughter, who married the 5th Earl of Haddington and handed on the Earldom of Rothes to her second son. Then followed Earl, Earl, Countess, Earl, Countess, Earl, Countess, Countess, Earl, Earl, the present being the 19th. But Leslie always rules as the family name.

XXXII

MINTO HOUSE, MINTO, ROXBURGHSHIRE

MINTO HOUSE is the seat of the 5th Earl of Minto, whose family name is Elliot, and who succeeded his father in 1914. He served in the Scots Guards and was promoted Captain in 1916. In 1921 he married Marion, daughter of G. W. Cook of Montreal. The house stands at the beginning of the slope which forms the northern side of the Cheviot Hills, and is only twelve miles from the border between Scotland and England. Place and name call up pictures of the Border Elliots and their raids.

In the fifteenth century the Chiefs of the Elliots were " of Redheugh," and were held responsible for good order in Liddesdale—no easy task when it is remembered that that was also the country of the Armstrongs. A branch of the Redheugh family was that " of Stobs," and it is from these Elliots that the Earl of Minto is descended.

The present Minto House was only completed in 1814 ; and its predecessor cannot be described, for it has been absorbed in the new house and its existence can be felt more than seen. The Earl who built it was the Governor-General of India, but he never saw it in its completed state, for it was in the year of its completion that he returned from India after seven years of service, and he died on his way from London to Scotland. So it was only his mortal remains which entered the house that he had built.

There had been a house on the site from an indefinite date, and as the old house was surrounded by a moat it must have had its origin far back in the days of defensive dwellings. Countess Anna Maria, wife of the 1st Earl, had added two wings and a storey in the latter half of the eighteenth century, so that no long time elapsed between her additions and the building of the present house. The architect was Archibald Elliot, who did much excellent work in his day.

Minto House has one great note—it is unusual. The note is apparent as we come to the end of the long avenue and obtain the first glimpse of the structure, with its two blocks at right angles and an arcaded porch curved outward filling up the interior part of the angled space. The roof of the porch, with a classical balustrade,

125

is supported on four rounded columns, while behind it a shorter curve of the masonry of the house is continued to the roof of the three-storeyed front, which has a plain parapet all the way along. The capitals of the columns are Ionic. The two lines which face north and east in the entrance view have their corresponding south and west fronts at the back of the house, with the joining angle shaped into octagon form of which three faces are visible. The ground plan is thus the old Scottish L, the longer limb being the south block, the other the west, and the total outside length of the letter about 320 feet.

There is a gradual rise of the ground to the north from the entrance front, with a fall to the south on the south side where a stream runs; and this slope gives a character to the garden and affects the architectural features. The wall which runs to the north on the east side, continuous with the line of the entrance front, contains a handsome wrought-iron gate, "the dogs of Minto" in stone guarding it on each side of the parapet. The gate was copied for Government House, Simla, when the late Lord Minto was Viceroy of India.

The configuration of the ground gives the west and south fronts a fourth storey, with a walk along both which is reached by a descent of a short flight of steps. On the south front the walk is on a terrace, from which the bank of the river slopes deep and steep. Near this point a charmingly placed bridge crosses the stream, from the other side of which a commanding and artistic view of the west and south fronts is obtained. Near the south-east end of the house is a very attractive pond surrounded by trees, above which the building towers at a most impressive height. The second Sir Gilbert Elliot, who was born in 1693 and died in 1766, planted these trees, placing on one side of the pond a row of larches, sent as seedlings by John, Duke of Argyll, and kept in pots in a hot-house until they were put into their present quarters, where some of them are now 100 feet high.

An avenue of beeches dates from the same period. The same Sir Gilbert added to the house, and removed the old village of Minto from a straggling position across the river from the house, and laid it out on Minto Green, preserving the old church, however, the ground around which is known as "the church garden."

An improvement made by the late Earl was the restoration of Fatlips Castle, which stands on a wild and tumbled mass of trap rocks overhanging the River Teviot to a height of 721 feet. Little is known of its history, except that tradition says that it was the stronghold of a turbulent Turnbull—one of the tribe which James IV.

MINTO HOUSE
FROM THE SOUTH-WEST

MINTO HOUSE
THE GARDEN GATE

found so troublesome to the peace of the Border that he hunted them until he compelled 200 of them to meet him with halters round their necks. Then he hanged some of them to encourage the others to be good. The Turnbull of Fatlips Castle is celebrated in Scott's *Lay of the Last Minstrel* :

> " On Minto's crags the moonbeams glint
> Where Barnhill hewed his bed of flint,
> Who flung his outlawed limbs to rest
> Where falcons hang their giddy nest."

The topography of the interior is rather puzzling to a stranger, as the entrance-hall and its extension " the round room " cut through the house from the angle of the entrance to the octagon angle at the back. Doors open from the two halls into rooms and short passages, and sometimes rooms are entered also from each other. The " round room " is lighted from a dome and " lantern " in the roof. Two rooms have names from special associations—the Heathfield room and the Scott room. Lord Heathfield was George Augustus Elliot, eighth son of the third Sir Gilbert Elliot of Stobs. He is famous for his wonderful defence of Gibraltar from July, 1779, till February, 1783 ; and the room receives its name from a painting of the hero which it contains. The Scott room is on the ground floor, just below the Heathfield room, and receives its name from a painting of Sir Walter Scott, done by Colvin Smith, to show his appreciation of permission given him by the Earl of the day to shoot over part of the grounds.

The lands of Minto have an ancient history, part having been granted by King Robert Bruce to Gulielmus Barbitonsor—whose name Latinists will recognise as meaning the " Beard-cutter," and who is accepted by some as belonging to the family of Barbour which gave Scotland an eminent poet. But the first real laird who appears in history is John Turnbull, of the year 1390, and the first Elliot laird is Sir Gilbert of the reign of James VI. He is known as " Gibbie o' the Gowden Gartens." His great-grandson, also Gilbert, was he who laid out the gardens and enlarged the house ; and this Gilbert's daughter Jean will always be remembered for her beautiful song, " The Flowers of the Forest." He bore the judicial title of Lord Minto, and is counted as the second Sir Gilbert Elliot of Minto. The fourth Sir Gilbert began the family connection with India, of which he was made Governor-General in 1808 ; and he was successively created Baron Minto, Viscount Melgund, and Earl of Minto, the last two in 1812.

Sir Walter Scott and Thomas Campbell were frequent visitors to Minto in the time of the first Earl, who was also a good friend to the poet John Leyden, a native of the neighbouring village of Denholm. Campbell wrote " Lochiel's Warning " in the old house. The famous lines—

> " 'Tis the sunset of life gives me mystical lore,
>   And coming events cast their shadows before,"

occurred to him after he had gone to bed. So he called a servant, had tea taken to him, and completed the poem.

The same Earl of Minto was a great friend of Admiral Lord Nelson, of whom the house has many relics. Among them is a large bundle of letters from the Admiral and Lady Hamilton, all of them full of interest, and at least one of them, from Lady Hamilton, very pathetic.

XXXIII

NEWBYTH, EAST FORTUNE, EAST LOTHIAN

IN East Lothian there is a kind of cluster of old-world towns and villages—Aberlady, East Linton, Longniddry, Dirleton, and several others—quaint and pretty, in extremely fine farming country, and generally looking comfortable. Of such places East Fortune is one, tucked away inland and sequestered. Near it is Newbyth, also sequestered. It is a fine estate, and the house is one of fine proportions, Gothic in design. The laird is Sir David Baird, Baronet, the fourth holder of the dignity.

The entrance to the house faces the west, and the front line of this part is that of the principal block. The whole house consists of two rectangular blocks, the other being joined to this at the north-east angle by a triangular extension with an arcaded front to the south. The extension contains the billiard-room, and the secondary block to the east of it contains the kitchen premises. The plan is, therefore, like two separate houses with a very narrow junction at the north-east angle of one block and the south-west angle of the other, where the arcade is.

The west front shows the Gothic features fully and simply. The whole block has octagonal towers of three storeys in height at the four angles, and the west front has two other towers of similar form, but more slender, which divide the front into three parts. The space between the slender towers contains the entrance, formed by Gothic arches and a narrow arcade. The whole of the frontage, two storeys high, is symmetrical, with windows which have the usual Gothic form, pointed within a square-headed moulding. There is a partly sunk storey which is continued on the other fronts, and all the way round the roof of the block is a crenellated parapet.

The south front has a great similarity to the west, the octagonal towers being similarly placed, but there is a little variation of the details of the centre, and there is no doorway. The east face is continuous from angle tower to angle tower, without intervening slender towers. On all the fronts there are string courses between the storeys, and slit windows in the towers.

The lawn on the south front is very extensive, divided into a multitude of flower-beds which in the summer and autumn are full of beautiful colours, with little of the merely conventional about them. There is a great area of grass lawn. With low boundary walls, plain and balustered parapets broken at intervals by little flights of steps in nooks and corners, with the trees which surround it, and with the views of the house from various positions of the lawn, the whole picture is delightful, and has an air of restful seclusion. On this side the owner has made a narrow clearing long in line among the trees, so that from the windows of the south front a view can be had of Traprain Law, a curious natural mound associated with King Loth and with St. Kentigern, whose other name is St. Mungo. Until the wonderful excavations conducted by the Society of Antiquaries of Scotland recently revealed the Mound as a site of several civilised but prehistoric settlements, the connection was mostly regarded as mythical. But the discoveries, fully described in *The Treasure of Traprain* by A. O. Curle, published in 1923, lend probability to the main points of the legend.

According to it, Loth was a King of Lothian with his seat in the neighbourhood. He had a daughter Thenew, who had a liaison, or, let us suppose and believe, a marriage contract with a neighbouring prince of whom her father did not approve. The father ordered her to be thrown from the rock, but she was miraculously saved and carried over to the neighbourhood of Culross in Fife, where St. Serf found her on the shore and tended her. She gave birth to a son, whom the old saint brought up and ultimately sent forth as an evangelist of the Faith to the west of Scotland, under the name of Kentigern, where he founded the city of Glasgow, and was known by the endearing term of Mungo.

The arcaded Gothic porch in the west front of the house gives entrance to a hall with a groined ceiling and a stone floor. A double door in a full Gothic doorway leads into the great hall, of which the first striking feature is its height, rising to the roof, where its principal lighting comes from a cupola or " lantern." Its Gothic arches are the next feature. On the ground floor they occupy the east side, and admit to another arcaded part from which various rooms are entered. In this part the ceiling is groined as in the hall, and it carries the gallery which goes round the inner hall on the first floor. On the north side of the inner hall a doorway gives access to the main stairway, and a passage leads first north and then west along the outline of the house to the secondary block.

In the front hall is a large case with a glass front and sides. It contains the gorgeous trappings of a horse, presented to the famous General Sir David Baird by the Pasha of Egypt. Another trophy is the sword of Tippoo Sultan, found in the Sultan's bed-chamber

NEWBYTH
FROM THE SOUTH-EAST

NEWBYTH
FROM THE SOUTH-WEST

after the capture of Seringapatam on May 4, 1799, and presented by the Army to Major-General Baird in admiration of his leadership of the storming party. The sword of Sir Colin Campbell, Lord Clyde, is also there.

The principal rooms are on the south front, so that the outlook is on the garden lawn and is receptive of all the sunshine which can be had. The morning-room is a very charming room, which has its original Chinese flowered wall-paper, now about 100 years old. The house was built towards the close of the eighteenth century, from designs by Robert and James Adam, famous for their classical designs. A writer on *The Architecture of Robert and James Adam*, published in 1922, expressed the view that the incursion of the brothers Adam into the Gothic style was not a success, but this house designed by them is undoubtedly a successful piece of work.

The drawing-room occupies the centre of the south front, and has in the overmantel a very interesting painting by Sir Francis Grant, P.R.A., from its containing portraits of a number of the original members of the old Golf Club at North Berwick—among them Lord Elcho, G. Wauchope, Carnegie, Stewart of Alderson, Macdonald of Clanranald, J. Campbell of Glensaddel, Sir David Baird, Captain Brown, R. Oliphant of Condie, and Colonel Norval. Most of them are on the putting-green and some are wearing tall hats ; Captain Brown is on his horse.

The east wall is largely taken up with Sir David Wilkie's painting of Sir David Baird finding the body of Tippoo, the attitude of the General " heroic."

The library is a very fine room in the south-east angle of the main block. It has a very handsome moulded plaster ceiling of interlacing geometrical forms. There is an overmantel painting of the hero of Seringapatam standing beside his charger. There are many family paintings, and an excellent collection of books. The dining-room is close to the triangular part, and has the disadvantage of being somewhat distant from the kitchen. But it is an excellent room, and interesting from its family paintings.

The name Newbyth, pronounced " Newbaith," comes from Aberdeenshire, where there is an old estate named Byth, and that Byth was the property of James Baird of Byth about the year 1600. His son was Sir John Baird of Newbyth, a Lord of Session with the judicial title of Lord Newbyth. James was to have been created Baron Doveran by Charles I., who had issued the Warrant, but was killed by the Cromwellians before a patent could be made out. The present owner of Newbyth is descended from him who had the Warrant without the patent.

Newbyth is the parish of Whitekirk to all intents and purposes, as Sir David owns the whole parish. It may be assumed that when his ancestor purchased the estate and wished to carry on the old Aberdeenshire name of Byth, he simply used the name Newbyth instead of Whitekirk; but Whitekirk remains the ecclesiastical entity, although it is united to the parish of Tyninghame. In the old days the Church and Manor of Whitekirk belonged to the Monks of Holyrood, and the church was a great resort of pilgrims. It was the shrine to which the widow of James I. professed to set out from Leith, when she really intended to make for Stirling Castle with her infant son James II.

XXXIV

NEWHAILES, MUSSELBURGH, MIDLOTHIAN

NEWHAILES HOUSE is not much over five miles east of Edinburgh, on the outskirts of the very ancient town of Musselburgh, of which the nearest part to Newhailes is still known by its old name of Fisherrow, which it had as a separate burgh, the successor of the old Roman port at the mouth of the River Esk. And from Newhailes can be seen across the river the church which crowns the hill of Inveresk, on which stood at one time a Roman prætorium.

The naturalness of the grounds of Newhailes House is their special note, but one which is disappearing, for building schemes are encroaching on them to some extent, though not greatly so far, and possibly they will leave the house with a large area untouched. An avenue leads off a long side road connecting main county roads. Leaving the avenue and turning to the right, one might believe himself in a wood, where stand some very fine trees. The avenue is only of moderate length, and at the end we find a very curious configuration: there is a wall in front of us, with a handsome gateway, through which we see the south front of the house. The wall stretches to left and right, curving towards the ends of the house, and both sides are ramparts rather than walls. On our left, near the house, a long passage runs under the rampart parallel with the west end of the house—quite a striking underground way leading to the kitchen side.

The result of this configuration is that the house is fronted by a large enclosed courtyard, consisting of a lawn encircled by a drive. The frontage is long, the lines broken only enough to relieve the eye from the feeling of monotony, and it is symmetrical in design, about 150 feet from end to end. The whole building is three storeys high; there is a centre part three windows wide, surmounted by a flat pediment. On the ground floor and the first floor the middle space is occupied by entrances, the lower more elaborate than the upper, for a porch with columns supports a stair on each side running up to the other door, which is the principal entrance. The ends of the line are slightly projecting wings, each three windows wide, and the parts between the wings and the centre are of similar width.

133

The whole front is plastered roughcast and largely covered with creepers. The back of the house is of almost the same description.

The name Newhailes suggests an old Hailes, and that old Hailes is to be found in Hailes Castle, of which the remains still stand not far from the main road to Dunbar. Hailes Castle was a stronghold which appears regularly in the measures of defence taken by Scotland against the invasions from England, and at one time it belonged to the Hepburns, the family of the Earl of Bothwell of Queen Mary's day. In the course of time it came into the hands of the family of Dalrymple, represented by the Earl of Stair of the present day. The first Viscount Stair was appointed a Lord of Session in the time of Cromwell, and was at a later date Lord President of the Court of Session. One of his younger sons, Sir David Dalrymple, Baronet, became the proprietor of Hailes, and is designated " of Hailes." It was he who became the possessor of Newhailes, the year being 1709, and it was an old house at the time.

It is sometimes stated that it was built by " Sir James Dalrymple, Baronet, a grandson of the first Earl of Stair," but this is a mistake in two directions—it was an old house, and the new name was given to it not by a grandson of the first Earl, but by a brother.

This is the true story. It had at one time the name of Whitehill, but was known as Burghton when Sir David bought it in 1709 from John, Lord Bellenden of Burghton, as was his style at the time. Sir David's portrait appears in a painting by Allan Ramsay in the library overmantel at Newhailes. It was to be Sir David's new residence instead of Hailes Castle, therefore he called it Newhailes. At an earlier period it had belonged to a family of the name of Preston, connected with the Prestons of Craigmillar, and one charter shows that they owned it as early as 1480. It was a modest country house, to which its new proprietor added largely at one end, while his son, Sir James Dalrymple, added to it at the other end. Sir James appears as a boy in the painting just mentioned, with his father. The chief portion of the first addition was the great library in which is the overmantel painting, and that forms the south end of the whole house on our right as we look at the entrance-front. It was afterwards filled with books by Sir James's son, Sir David, the eminent judge and man of letters who is known by his judicial title of Lord Hailes, and who died in 1792. It is interesting to know that so far as the books are concerned the library remains today as that famous and literary Lord Hailes left it. I have often looked through the books as they lie on the shelves in which Lord Hailes placed them.

The internal arrangement of the house is very simple and at the same time very interesting. The mention of the great library makes

NEWHAILES
THE SOUTH FRONT

| JOHN, | JAMES, | FIELD-MARSHAL JOHN, |
| FIRST EARL OF STAIR | FIRST VISCOUNT STAIR | SECOND EARL OF STAIR |

NEWHAILES
PORTRAITS IN THE DINING-ROOM

a useful starting-point. From that east wing right on to the west wing there is a continuous passage, each of the wings entered by a door, but the other rooms open to the passage. The library serves the purpose of a drawing-room, and contains chairs covered with pictured tapestry. The fireplace is of beautiful Italian design with many different marbles. The old " dog grate," the floral and ribbon decorations, and the fine painting above, all combine to give the room an air of old-world distinction. On either side of the fireplace is a landscape by Thomson of Duddingston, the parson-painter, one representing Tantallon Castle with the sea washing against the rocks, and the other Hailes Castle with a mountain background.

The room next to it is the small library, with paintings of the judge known as Lord Drummore, who died in 1755; Sir David Dalrymple who bought the house ; the other Sir David, Lord Hailes ; Sir Hew Dalrymple, third son of the first Viscount Stair, and founder of the North Berwick branch of the family; and Sir James Dalrymple, M.P. This room contains chairs which formed a model for Her Majesty the Queen's chairs at Holyrood Palace.

The next, which is the middle division, is the entrance-hall, extending back to the north face of the house, from which a single stair descends to the grounds. And then, to the west of the hall, is the dining-room. This room is distinguished by fluted columns supporting the ceiling towards the west, while the east wall, containing the fireplace, has a painting of the first Viscount above it. To the left of it is one of his son, the 1st Earl, who was the Glencoe Earl, and both of these are by Sir John de Medina. On the other side is the famous Field-Marshal, the 2nd Earl, by Allan Ramsay. The room at the west end, the wing added by the son of the first Dalrymple owner, is a study which was used by the late Sir Charles Dalrymple, Baronet, for about twenty years M.P. for Ipswich.

The most distinguished personage of all these owners of Newhailes was Lord Hailes, the eldest of sixteen children. He was not a success as an oral pleader on account of a defect in articulation. But in his day a great deal of the work of the Scottish Bar was done by written pleadings, and in these his knowledge of Law and History, combined with a gift of clear exposition, gave him great success.

One of the most prominent notes of his character was his reverence for sacred things, which made him one of the most effective opponents of David Hume's teaching, and attracted him to Dr. Samuel Johnson without having met him. It was Lord Hailes who recommended James Boswell to seek the acquaintance of

Johnson, for which the world of literature is indebted to him. Hailes and Johnson met at last during the Doctor's tour of Scotland in 1773. Lord Hailes died in 1792, and Newhailes passed through his daughter Jean to a Fergusson of Kilkerran, who added the name Dalrymple. His second son inherited Newhailes, and was the late Sir Charles Dalrymple, already mentioned, who received a baronetcy. His son is another Sir David Dalrymple.

XXXV

NIDDRIE MARISCHAL, LIBERTON, MIDLOTHIAN

FROM the historic Holyrood to the historic Craigmillar Castle is no long distance, and from Craigmillar Castle to Niddrie Marischal is an easy short walk. It is a house with a long history, and it is only about three miles from Edinburgh Castle. The entrance-gates and lodge are in the Gothic style, Tudor or Jacobean, and admit to a long and broad avenue by which the house is reached. The north front is that which we approach, and it contains the entrance. The first impression is that of the old Scottish L-shaped castle, as we find a line of buildings on our left at right angles to the main front. Probably it is more a matter of convenience than of design, although it looks as if that part is old, formerly detached, and ultimately joined to the main part by filling up the intervening space.

The general character of the north front is that of two square towers forming the ends of a line, with a central part receding from the line of the towers, and this central part containing a Gothic porch thrown well forward. The centre part is two storeys in height, the tower on the left of the line is three storeys, and that on the right is one storey higher. All the front is reminiscent of the days when a house had to be capable of defence, and it is surmounted by a battlemented parapet. The right-hand tower has beautiful broken corbelling all round the base of the parapet, and the other tower has a front line of corbelling copied from the former.

The tower on the right is the oldest part of the present building, and is a genuine " keep," believed to be about 300 years old. It was built in consequence of the burning of the former house by an Edinburgh mob, and the story of the causes which gathered that mob is a strange record of evil and of retribution.

The estate has been in the hands of the family of Wauchope more than 500 years, and the house which preceded this must have been one of real grandeur. A manuscript notebook belonging to the house and containing much interesting matter tells that the old house was capable of accommodating one hundred strangers. The cause of the burning is to be found in the evil courses of Archibald Wauchope, " the young Laird of Nidrie," who is so often mentioned in Calderwood's *History of the Kirk of Scotland*. At the time of the burning, however, the estate had been forfeited, and had passed to Sir James Sandilands, of Slamannan, who is believed to have built the keep, and who sold the estate in 1608 to his son-in-law, Sir Francis Wauchope, son of the forfeited Archibald.

One of the most popular of the sentimental songs of our language, " Annie Laurie," owes its present form to Lady John Scott, whose mother was a Wauchope of Niddrie. The original was by Douglas of Fingland, two eight-line stanzas, of which the first was practically that of the song as it is now. The second ran thus :

> " She's backit like a peacock,
> She's breistit like a swan,
> She's jimp about the middle,
> Her waist ye weel may span.
> Her waist ye weel may span,
> And she has a rolling eye,
> And for bonnie Annie Laurie
> I'd lay down my head and die."

Lady John Scott altered this verse, added a third, and composed the melody.

The tower stands on a surface about 22 feet square, and rises to a height of about 50 feet. It has a platform roof arched with stone. The original entrance into the keep was on the north side, but that entrance has been built up, and is now covered by a stone buttress which rises to the middle of the third storey. The date may be taken as 1600; the small centre addition on the north belongs to 1636; and the other alterations and additions belong to the approximate date of 1790. William Adam is stated to have been the architect of those alterations and additions, but as he died in 1748 it is hardly likely that he had planned them, and it is more likely that his sons Robert and James were the architects.

When the extension of 1636 was made the keep was altered internally. Practically only the four walls and the vaulted roof were left, the interior being used for the great stair which was to lead to the extension. The stair and its landing are said by an architectural authority to be one of the finest works of the kind left to Scotland.

The contrasts in the periods of building are to be seen on both the north and the south fronts, the modern note asserting itself much more on the south, where the eastern Adam part shows large bay windows of many lights, while the windows to the west are ordinary single lights. That western part has evidently been raised

NIDDRIE MARISCHAL
THE SOUTH FRONT

NIDDRIE MARISCHAL
THE NORTH FRONT

one storey, taking in windows which were formerly dormers with pediments. The centre dormer of the three has the date 1636 on it; that to the west has two sets of initials, " S.F.W." and " D.I.S. "; while that to the east has " S.J.W." and " D.A.H." These carvings indicate the completion of that part begun by Sir Francis Wauchope and his wife Dame Jean Sandilands, and finished by his son, Sir John Wauchope, whose wife was Dame Anna Hamilton.

The main eastern part is built in the castellated style, presenting some of the features of the old keep and having a parapet with embrasures. It extends to the south on a line about 90 feet long, and has the library to the north and the drawing-room to the south, with one of the bay windows mentioned above. The total east line, including the old, almost detached, part, extends to about 110 feet, almost the length of the south line.

The Wauchopes are said to have come from France in 1062, and they held their lands originally from the Keiths, Earls Marischal, for whom they acted as baillies. A mound known as the " Law Knowe," a little east of the house, seems to denote a " moot hill " and judiciary powers on this part. Gilbert Wauchope had a charter of Niddrie from Robert III., and the names of Patrick Wauchope and his spouse Isobel appear in a deed of November 6, 1479. The late General Andrew Gilbert Wauchope, of Niddrie Marischal, was known and loved for his fine qualities as a soldier and a Christian gentleman. He was killed in command of the Highland Brigade at the Battle of the Modder River on December 11, 1899, leading what was intended to be a surprise attack under cover of darkness at Magersfontein. He left no heir, and his widow, a daughter of the late Sir William Muir, K.C.S.I., is the mistress of the historic house and lands.

The outer hall is almost square, and gives access by a door on the left to the small old block. In front, steps lead to the handsome room known as the Hall, extending from the north to the south front and opening there upon a balcony. It also extends west into the " keep," where the dark oak stair rises in three sections to a landing which, being open to the hall, forms a gallery overlooking it. From the gallery hangs a white flag with a blue centre and Arabic letters. It was captured at Omdurman, and presented by Brigadier-General Hector Macdonald to the late General Wauchope.

The dining-room is entered from this hall on the right, and the drawing-room from the opposite side. The inner wall of the dining-room is evidently the former outer wall of the " keep," and one of its charms is its oak panelling, with paintings of Wauchopes inset all round the room. The drawing-room is a beautiful room about

40 feet long, with a plaster ceiling panelled. It contains among many portraits one of the late General. The library is entered from the north end of the drawing-room and also from the hall.

The appearance of the house is greatly enhanced by the charm of the grounds on the south. On the south and east sides there is a terrace, from which the ground slopes down to the Burdiehouse Burn. The lower level is reached below the balcony by a flight of steps, and similar steps are on the east side. There is a long " rose walk," which is also called " Queen Mary's Walk " from the circumstance that Queen Mary often visited Niddrie when she stayed at Craigmillar Castle.

There was in ancient days a chapel at the west end of the mansion, founded in 1387 by Robert Wauchope, but destroyed in 1688 by the same Edinburgh mob which destroyed Holyrood Abbey Church. All that can be said to remain of it is the old tomb at the west end adjoining the wall of the dining-room—with the inscription: " This tome ves biggit be Robert Vauchope of Nydry Marischal, and enteris heir, P.P. 1587." There is a further inscription round the slab to the memory of the builder's father William, who died in 1587.

XXXVI

OXENFOORD CASTLE, CRANSTON, MIDLOTHIAN

THE present aspect of Oxenfoord Castle, which is a magnificent pile in the parish of Cranston, Midlothian, dates from the year 1842, when it received a new front. But it belongs to several ages, and it has had three modern stages of restoration and improvement. The stage which preceded that of 1842 belongs to the year 1782, when, according to *Seats of the Nobility and Gentry in Great Britain and Wales*, published in 1787, the architect Robert Adam " preserved the old apartments, and by his inventive power removed all the deformities and substituted in their stead beauties similar to those which he introduced in Sion House, Middlesex."

The ancient building was so old and yet so good in the reign of Charles II. that it was then rebuilt. The following account appeared in the *Edinburgh Magazine* of 1785, and is quoted in *An Account of Oxenfoord Castle*, compiled by the Honourable Hew Hamilton Dalrymple, and privately printed in 1901 : " The ancient castle was rebuilt in the reign of Charles II. by the Viscount of Oxfuird, upon a plan given by the Duke of Lauderdale, in which were several very good rooms, and a noble one 50 feet long ; but the outward appearance of the house was very awkward and irregular."

The description further says : " King James, when Duke of York, and the Princess Anne, when they were in Scotland, used to stay for weeks in this castle on visits; and some of the furniture of the rooms in which they slept is still preserved." It was 100 feet long, the middle part 50 broad and 60 high. With these figures, we can gather that the house as it left the hands of the brothers Adam would consist of a square castellated block with a side about 50 feet long, having a slender circular tower at each angle, the front facing the north as now. To the west would be a smaller and lower extension, while on the east the drawing-room block would extend from south to north. This form is not at once evident now, because the present front was added in 1842 by John, 8th Earl of Stair, from plans by William Burn. That front, which is the north, comprises only a single storey and basement, with the end of the library as added by Burn; but it extends considerably to the west of the older building,

141

the extension having a large court behind it. Consequently, there is a very imposing north line of about 165 feet.

The castle, therefore, belongs to four periods, the oldest house without a definite date, but very old. Practically nothing is known of its history before the time of Charles II.

The avenue is long and handsome, rising as it draws near the house. There is a deep depression to the north, and the hollow is crossed by a bridge which carries the avenue. The great central structure towers above the house and has on its roof, in stone, the bull and the horse, heraldic supporters of the arms of the Viscounts of Oxfuird. To the right is the lower extension, and to the left is the block stretching from north to south and containing the library and drawing-room. The front which Burn added followed the design of the Adams very faithfully.

The south front has the most impressive aspect of all the parts. It rises to a height of four storeys above the basement, while the angle turrets have an additional storey. The wings are lower, but still high, the western extremity terminated by a square tower-like wing containing three fine windows in a continuous bay, all set in rectangular frames, mullioned and transomed after the Jacobean style. On the east and south sides there is much delicate corbelling, while the wide outward curve of the wall between the angle turrets of the south enhances the general appearance of dignity.

The yew hedges which enclose the flower garden on the east side are very interesting, trimmed into a form which harmonises with the style of the house. There are two sundials, one on the east side very old. It comprises three blocks, of which the lowest is modern. The topmost contains three dial faces, and the middle stone has on each of its four faces a bear sculptured rampant—which a well-known architectural work describes erroneously as evidently the crest of the MacGills of Cousland. Their crest was a phœnix in flames; and the sundial was removed from Remote Farm, to which it had been taken from Cranston.

On entering the house from the north there is an outer hall adorned with pistols, swords, spears, and other weapons. On the left are a few steps, and then more on the right, leading to an inner hall, on the way to which some curious old curling-stones are seen. Then there is the billiard-room, with a fireplace designed by the Adams. Above the fireplace is " King James's Mirror," presented by King James VI. to Viscount Oxfuird, who had so often entertained him. Among the paintings are a " Holy Family " by Callot, and a group of figures by Watteau. Among the family portraits are the first Viscount Stair and his son the first Earl.

OXENFOORD CASTLE
FROM THE SOUTH-EAST

OXENFOORD CASTLE
FROM THE WEST

The billiard-room is a kind of corridor, but behind it is an inner corridor, with a staircase leading to the upper rooms. The drawing-room is entered from the inner corridor, and is specially beautiful. It is divided from the library by folding doors, which are usually open; and the measurement of what is practically one great room is about 90 feet in length, without including window space. Both rooms have beautiful ceilings. The library was built by Burn and the drawing-room by Adam, but probably Burn altered the drawing-room ceiling.

Over the oak bookcases of the library hang paintings of many famous people—Andrew Fletcher of Saltoun, the political writer; the Honourable Sir James Dalrymple, Baronet, of Borthwick, an antiquary; Hew Dalrymple, Lord Drummore, a judge; Robert MacGill, 2nd Viscount of Oxfuird, by Sir Peter Lely; Montesquieu; and many others. The library contains the manuscript correspondence of F.-M. the 2nd Earl of Stair, and some volumes of Oxenfoord and Haddington papers—these things in addition to valuable books.

The drawing-room has a handsome marble fireplace, the mantel supported by Caryatides, and the under-mantel decorated with festoons of flowers. Among the paintings are " Tantallon Castle " and " Castle Urquhart " by Thomson of Duddingston, a large landscape by Moucheron, and a shipping picture by W. van der Velde dated 1671.

The dining-room has a very special interest because it is in the oldest part of the house. It is more than 65 feet in length from west to east, and it occupies the large curve in the south wall, thus having a very fine window. The plaster walls are made to look like oak, and some of the paintings are in panels on the north and west walls, but done on canvas. The ceiling is by the Adams. Two cupboards on the fireplace side of the room, in the wall which separates the dining-room from the drawing-room on the east, are rather curious, for it is evident that they were windows of the old castle. Under the dining-room are some excellent rooms with the vaulted ceilings which delight the antiquary.

In the remote long-ago there were two baronies, Upper Cranston and Nether Cranston, of which the former gave name to the family which ultimately bore the title Lord Cranstoun. The other barony came to be called Cranstoun Riddel after it had become the property of the family of Riddel. The Riddels parted with it in the reign of David II., and it passed through several hands before it became the property of David MacGill, King's Advocate in 1582. His grandson James became Viscount of Oxfuird and Lord MacGill of Cousland in 1651. Male heirs failed after the second lord, and his daughter assumed the titles and married the third son of the Earl of Lauderdale. Her son was allowed the titles but died without issue, and then his mother's sister assumed them with the estates. The next heir was Thomas Hamilton of Fala, descended from a daughter of the 1st Viscount; and Thomas Hamilton married a daughter of Sir John Dalrymple of Cousland. Their daughter, Elizabeth Hamilton MacGill, succeeded to Fala and Oxenfoord, and married her cousin John Dalrymple, younger of Cousland, a descendant of the second son of the 1st Viscount Stair. Their son, the 5th Baronet of Cousland, succeeded as 8th Earl of Stair in 1840, and was followed by his brother as 9th Earl.

The Dalrymple family is derived from Dalrymple in Ayrshire, whence they obtained their name before the time of King David II. The Dalrymples of Stair in Ayrshire appear in history as early as the reign of James IV., and there are many complications and interchanges between the families of Dalrymple and Kennedy before " Dalrymple of Stair " became a finality. The present Earl of Stair is the 12th, was M.P. before the War, was wounded and taken prisoner in the retreat from Mons, and in 1917 was allowed to pass into internment in Switzerland.

XXXVII

PINKIE HOUSE, MUSSELBURGH, MIDLOTHIAN

AT the east end of the town of Musselburgh, which is older
than Edinburgh and was a Roman Station, stand the entrance
gates of Pinkie House. They stand where two tall columns
look as though they carried of old the gates of the town on that side ;
but that is a delusion—the impressive columns are the remains of a
turnpike gate. Yet they are interesting as marking also the site
of the ancient " East Port " of the town, at which dues were levied on
produce entering the burgh. For

> " Musselburgh wes a burgh when Edinburgh wes nane,
> And Musselburgh wol be a burgh when Edinburgh's gane—"

a rather proud and empty boast.

The avenue is not long, and a glimpse of the house may be had
from the gateway. Its origin lies back into the centuries and is not
definitely known ; but it is supposed to have had its beginning about
the year 1190. It was a part of the possessions of the Abbey of
Dunfermline, and as that abbey was founded in 1072 the date 1190
is not improbable for Pinkie House, which began as an ecclesiastical
House. The first part was the square tower or " keep," which is still
the central feature, and probably there were detached buildings
also. It is often spoken of as a rest-house for the monks of Dunfermline, but the strength of the "keep" rather indicates, in its earlier days,
a place of strength for the protection of its tenants and its rents. A
detached building existed at a later period to the south, and was
finally embodied in the building as it is now.

The modern history of the house begins with Alexander Seton,
fourth son of the 7th Lord Seton, and a younger brother of the
1st Earl of Winton. Alexander became Earl of Dunfermline, and was
the owner also of Fyvie Castle in Aberdeenshire. Pinkie came into
his possession with the lands of the Abbey, which were erected into
the Earldom for him. The 4th Earl was forfeited in 1690, but
Pinkie had passed from him shortly before, when it was bought by
the Marquis of Tweeddale. It changed hands again in 1788, the
purchaser being Sir Archibald Hope, Baronet, of Craighall ; and the

L

present laird is his great-great-grandson, another Sir Archibald, and a minor.

At present the house is of the familiar Scottish form, the L shape, one block facing east and the other facing south, and joined at a south-east angle, the interior fronts being therefore west and north. The principal entrance is in the west front, in which the old tower is the central part. There is in existence in the family papers a deed which states that the tower was built in 1390, which may perhaps be reconciled with the earlier date of tradition by assuming a smaller and earlier tower to which an addition was made. From the tower to the north end of that east block is the oldest part of the whole structure, and it is just possible that the Abbot of 1390 built it all. The length of the east block is about 148 feet now, and that of the south block is 125 feet.

The chronicles of the Dunfermline family say of Chancellor Seton : " He acquired the lands of Pinkie, where he built ane noble house, brave stone dykes about the garden and orchard, with other commendable policie about it." The west front has an inscription which gives the date : " Dominus Alexander Setonius, hanc domum ædificavit, non ad animi, sed fortunarum et agelli modum, 1613." The inscription is concealed now by the modern portion of the front which contains the porch. It is practically certain that the Chancellor was in possession before that date, and was busy with stone and lime. His initials appear on one side of a garden gateway, with the number 57, his age ; while the initials of his third wife appear on the other, with her age, 21. The date 1612 is thus furnished for that wall. The Chancellor's full intention seems to have been to fill in the north and west sides of a courtyard with walls ; I have seen the remains of the north wall, but I doubt if the west wall ever existed. In the great tower is an entrance to the second floor, and the other parts are reached by a wheel stair in a turret.

These stairs are only subsidiary now. The main staircase is to be found more than half-way towards the south end of the block, and is reached by a wide Gothic porch to the right of the tower giving entrance to a hall which is extended to the right until it ends in a doorway in the south wall giving access to the gardens. On the right of the passage, about the middle, rises a very handsome wide staircase to the first floor, after which a maze of passages and stairs communicates with a great number of interesting rooms in a house which has not been modernised out of its old-time memories.

The Earl built a beautiful well-canopy in the centre of what he intended to be his courtyard, and that remains a matter of interest

PINKIE HOUSE
THE ENTRANCE FRONT

PINKIE HOUSE
THE GALLERY, LOOKING NORTH

to antiquarians and Latinists—to Latinists because of its inscription, which goes all round the frieze of the canopy. Writers follow one another in saying that it is a quotation from Horace, but I have not found one who gives the reference or suggests the proper sequence of the words. So I have done my best to settle the matter by a search of Horace and an examination of the four sides of the structure. The inscription is, as far as I can make out, an elegiac hexameter couplet :

" Fŏn-te hŏc | frig-ĭ-dĭ | -ōr qŭo | nōn-vēl | pūr-ĭ-ŏr | ăl-tēr
Ĕt căp-ĭ | -ti ēt mēm | -bris | ū-til-ĭs | ūn-dă flŭ | -ĭt."

And the meaning is : " From this fountain, than which there is none other either cooler or purer, flows a stream useful for head and limbs." The word "fonte" is on the south side ; and, having picked it up, it is only necessary to read round by the east. The words are not a quotation from Horace, but an echo of his sentiment in two places, of which the clearer is from *Epistles*, Book I., Epistle XVI., lines 12, 13, 14 :

" Fons etiam rivo dare nomen idoneus, ut nec
Frigidior Thracam nec purior ambiat Hebrus,
Infirmo capiti fluit utilis, utilis alvo."

The meaning is : " A spring, worthy indeed to give name to a stream, flows useful to a weak head and stomach, for neither cooler nor purer does the Hebrus meander through Thracia."

Few Scottish houses have so many striking and beautiful architectural features blended so harmoniously—on the west side square tower and rounded bartizans, crow-stepped gable, Jacobean window over the porch, string courses and battlemented parapet : on the north face of the south wing some similar features, and indications which are realised by vaulted ceilings within. On the east front the row of tall stone chimney stacks is a feature in itself; and that north block, with a beautiful variety of Scottish features in the narrow north end, has what was once the most nearly perfect ascending series of oriel windows in Scotland, on its south end. The topmost of three has two transoms in each of its three divisions, the three sides of an octagon bay; the window below has one transom similarly; and that on the ground floor had no transom. Consequently, their sizes and horizontal divisions went from the bottom upwards on the arithmetical progression 1, 2, 3, the lowest window being very small. When it was decided, a long time ago, to turn this badly lighted room into a well-lighted dining-room the beautiful masonry was removed and a large window with solid stonework substituted. An artist in stone would have enlarged the window by making it a duplicate of the topmost, and that could yet be done.

The topmost window is that of the most remarkable room in the house, known as " the Pinkie Gallery " or " the Blue Room." It is 85 feet long, 19 broad, and it is unique in Scotland, displaying evidence of being the work of Italian artists. The ceiling is the finest of the Scottish pictorial ceilings, of which other examples are at Nunraw in East Lothian and Stobhall in Perthshire. The only way in which to obtain an adequate idea of the ceiling pictures is to lie on the floor and gaze upward—which I have done. Pictorial proverbs, Latin expressions of them, coats of arms, and a centre panel with the Dunfermline arms and the Earl's initials A.E.D., give material for long study. The room below the gallery is the drawing-room.

About an old house like this one would expect to have many ghosts, and that at least one of the good brothers of Dunfermline might " walk." But no ! Only occasionally is a lady seen, and no one knows who " Green Jean " is. She is sometimes accompanied by a child, and I know of no specific instance of anyone having seen the lady. But I know of one man who was much disturbed by the child entering his room repeatedly until he willed her to go away, and not come back. The man was very sensible; and so was the child !

XXXVIII

PITREAVIE CASTLE, DUNFERMLINE, FIFE

THE road by which Pitreavie Castle is approached is now one of the finest traffic roads in Scotland, due initially to improvements which were made necessary by the development of the Naval Base at Rosyth, near Dunfermline. The main avenue to Pitreavie, the lodge, and the entrance gates were removed to allow of the widening of the road. Half-way up the avenue is an old archway, between which and the castle is the " Beech Avenue," leading up to the north front of the house. The trend of the ground is a rise from south to north, and the rising ground to the north of the house is covered with trees, so that it is difficult to get a view of that front of the house without ascending the slope, so near are the bank and the trees to it. Although it has been for many generations out of the family which built it—the Wardlaws—it is still associated with the name, for Sir Henry Wardlaw, the 19th Baronet, although he lives in London, is " of Pitreavie," according to the original gift of the dignity, and he is so designated in Burke's *Peerage and Baronetage*.

The family of Beveridge now own it, Mr. Henry Beveridge having bought it in 1884 and made such additions to it that it is now a large house from having been one of only moderate size. But the family of Wardlaw ceased to be proprietors long years ago.

As a general description it may be said that the house is a long rectangle, narrow for its length, which is about 120 feet, while its width, except at the west end, may be said to be about 33 feet. Approximately at the centre of the north front, but more to the east than the west, the line is broken by a modern porch of real artistic merit. The west end, which is on our right as we look at the north front, projects forward considerably, and this end is a most interesting part of the original house. Above the porch, but well behind it, rises a handsome projection from the general line. It has a straight-line gable, and is evidently a part of the old house; but all to the left of that on this front is new. We are able to form an intelligible view of the form of the old house, which has not been swallowed up by the additions.

The porch is almost square in form, with a classical balustrade and a very ornate doorway, of which the jambs have a continuous

149

floral design. Above the frieze is a pediment with the Beveridge crest and scroll. The frieze carries the date " 1885," separating the initials " H.B." The gabled part has a fine window in it, corresponding in height with the first and second floors. From the porch a straight wall runs east, enclosing a small courtyard in front of the east addition. The east wing, though very modern in date, conserves the old ideas without affectation, and is not a mere imitation, for various details of the new part are plainly not of the old. The gabled top keeps it in harmony with the wing at the other end.

From the rising ground opposite the north front we can distinguish clearly between the old castle and its extension. If the middle gable was built exactly the same as the rest of the castle, the old house was of the shape of a capital E without the middle line, and this present middle gable was the east end of the line. The space between the two gables was a courtyard, with a completing wall which does not now exist ; a little further consideration will lead to the belief that the present middle gable was in its time an addition ; and we get back to the older Scottish form of the L-shaped house. The gateway of the courtyard survives, but in a different position. Above it are the Wardlaw arms, with a monogram containing the initials D.E. and W., conjectured to be those of Lady Wardlaw, the D. standing for " Dame."

In each of the junction angles of the E form is a round tower, rising at first from the foundations in a kind of round buttress, on which at the height of one storey are thrown out four lines of concentric corbelling which give the towers a greater diameter. The towers rise to the full height of the house and have conical roofs. Just beside the round tower on our left is the old principal entrance, within which is a small arched recess fitted with stone seats, said by tradition to be for the use of beggars—probably true, as the old kitchen was so near.

The old doorway is rectangular, with a double moulding round it and a pediment above. The tympanum is highly decorated with designs of leaves and fruit at the sides, while the centre has the initials " H.W." with the letter " S " above them, and holding them suspended by curious wreaths which have been described as " root-like," but are more like the legs of a bee. Above the apex of the pediment is the crest of the Wardlaws, a five-pointed star. Behind the door is the old iron " yett," with interlacing bars, vertical and horizontal. The ground floor of the old house was fully vaulted, and the doorway led through vaulted passages into vaulted rooms. In the alterations of 1885 it was desired to retain the drawing-room in this old part, but in order to give that room greater height it was

PITREAVIE CASTLE
THE NORTH FRONT

PITREAVIE CASTLE
THE OLD DOORWAY

found necessary to remove a large part of the vaulting below. This, of course, was a great pity from the point of view of the antiquarian; but the most interesting room on the ground floor, the kitchen, with the passage leading to it, was spared the interference, and it remains as a gunroom, with its fine old fireplace. The ancient wrought-iron grate is in the Antiquarian Museum in the Dunfermline Abbey buildings.

The one thing which can be said with certainty as to the date of the building of the old house is that it was before 1644, for that date is on the magnificent sundial which stands on the south front. As originally placed it had a flight of stone steps rising to it, and a wide octagonal paved space round it. Now it stands on an octagonal foundation, upon which is a square slab. The whole is about 6 feet high, and the dial part is very elaborate. The east face has the initials H.W. with the S. above ; the south face has a heart-shaped shield with the Wardlaw arms ; and the west face has a heart-shaped design.

The modern doorway leads us through an outer and an inner hall to a new feature in a corridor which runs west and east from the new wing to the old. It has a ceiling arched on both sides, with a flat centre. There is an oak staircase, and wall frescoes done in *tempera* in 1894 by C. H. Mackie—all subject pictures in the mediæval style. There used to be some fine tapestries in the old dining-room, now the drawing-room, but they are now at Fordel Castle. The drawing-room in the old west wing has a great bay window on the south and an oriel on the west—features in themselves.

The Wardlaws are said to have come from Saxony in the sixth century to England, and to derive their name from an office which they held under the Anglo-Saxon Kings. There were three leading branches in Scotland, those of Torrie, Luscar, and Balmule. Walter de Wardlaw was Bishop of Glasgow in 1368, and in 1385 he was made a Cardinal—the first in Scotland. His nephew Henry was appointed Bishop of St. Andrews about 1401, and founded the University of St. Andrews—the first in Scotland—in 1411. An old stone with the Bishop's arms and his initials " H.W."—also those of the founder of Pitreavie—was placed in 1909 in a reconstructed archway in the quadrangle of St. Mary's College.

The builder of Pitreavie was the eldest son of Sir Cuthbert Wardlaw of Balmule, and was Chamberlain to Queen Anne, the Danish wife of James VI. When James became King of England he made Sir Henry Wardlaw the Warden of the Palace of Dunfermline.

The family did not long hold Pitreavie, and this misfortune is associated in an old tradition with the battle of Inverkeithing in 1651, when Cromwell defeated the Scots with great slaughter near Pitreavie. The Clan Maclean suffered greatly in that battle, and it is said that a remnant of them who sought refuge in the castle had stones thrown on them from the roof by order of the laird. Hence the Wardlaws " went off like snow off a dyke." The castle then went to the Blackwood family, from one of whom Henry Beveridge bought it.

XXXIX

PRESTONFIELD, EDINBURGH

PRESTONFIELD is an old country house, but Edinburgh has grown out to it so much and is now so near it that to describe it as "Prestonfield, Midlothian" would not locate it. It is not the first house to stand on the site, but its predecessor disappeared entirely in the year 1680, having been burnt to the ground one night while the owner, Sir James Dick, Lord Provost of Edinburgh, was at a meeting of Magistrates. Sir James was a new Baronet, having received the honour in 1676, and he was believed to be in high favour with King Charles II. and the Duke of York. There had been anti-Papal riots in Edinburgh, in which the students of the University had taken a part, and the Lord Provost had dealt very firmly with the offenders. So it was believed that the burning of his house was a reprisal. Before he bought it, the house was known as Priestfield and belonged to the family of Hamilton; but Sir James changed the name to Prestonfield. Probably the old name denoted the lands to be old ecclesiastical possessions.

The Government and the Magistrates of Edinburgh decided to make good Sir James's loss, and he is believed to have received about £400 out of a sum of £800 promised. However, in 1687 he built the present house, which was designed by Sir William Bruce.

Its situation is almost due south of Edinburgh, and the houses of Edinburgh now reach within a few paces of it, while tramway cars and omnibuses almost pass it. Arthur's Seat towers above it on the north or north-east, with Samson's Ribs, a part of the hill, very prominent, and Duddingston Loch, now a bird sanctuary, a little to the north-east. There is an old prophecy that when Edinburgh shall surround Arthur's Seat, then shall the hill burst into flame. The condition is now almost fulfilled ; but probably respect for the prophecy will preserve a gap, more especially as it is well known that Arthur's Seat is the surviving hard core of a volcanic vent.

At the time when Sir James Dick bought the house and lands the ground was very swampy on account of its nearness to the hill, which poured its drainage down upon a property which had no effective system of carrying it away. But Sir James set to work to improve this. He made an arrangement with the city by which he collected all the street refuse for his property. With that and drainage he turned his lands to good account ; and the house which he built is beautiful.

The principal front is on the west, and displays an old-fashioned dwelling, the walls of which are " harled " throughout. The west front looks like two wings of similar design, each surmounted by a gable top of curved classical lines instead of the older style of crow-steps. Just below the curved lines the two wings are joined to present a frontage of even face. The part which forms the joining has a flat roof with a classical balustrade in front of it ; but this roof is only a small space, with sloping roofs on all except the balustrade sides.

Below this centre is a portico of which the canopy is almost square, with a width of 22 feet. The canopy has slender balusters, two pairs of flat pilasters supporting it at the back, and two pairs of smooth rounded columns in front, all the capitals Doric. On account of the trend of the ground downward from the west front on all sides the north and south fronts show four storeys instead of the three of the west front. Each of the two fronts mentioned has its own distinctive features. The south front has three windows on each floor, those of the topmost row ornamented by beautiful open pediments which lie on the roof line, each pediment differing in outline from the others. The north front has its outline broken by a central projection ascending from the ground to a height of a storey above the general level, with a gable of curved line.

On the east there is an extension which is much lower than the main house, both in level and in height. It presents the curious form of a circular outline to north and south, with a connecting part, still lower, which has a line curving outward to the east. It contains on the north side the ordinary dining-room and on the south the great dining-room on the ground floor, while above are the two drawing-rooms known as the " tapestry " room and the " leather " room. The extension does not appear to be of later date than the front, but the unusual combination of designs makes it seem possible that enough of the walls of the burnt-out house remained to influence the ground plan of the front part.

The interior of the house even exceeds the exterior in interest and beauty. The square vestibule is only the entering part of a corridor about 100 feet long, and extending from the front to the back. At a short distance from the entrance it rises by six steps, and a little further on it has fluted columns which mark the termination of the front block. Between the steps and the columns, on our left, rises the main staircase, which gives access to a gallery on the

PRESTONFIELD
FROM THE SOUTH-WEST

PRESTONFIELD
THE SOUTH FRONT

first floor, overlooking the corridor, and with a balustrade. The tapestry-room and the leather-room are entered from the gallery, and the former was decorated by the workmen who decorated Holyrood. The leather-room receives its name from its being panelled in old Cordova leather with a red ground, the ornamentation consisting of cupids and fruit in green, copper, and gold. These are believed to be the only remains of the house which the Edinburgh mob burned.

The most interesting room on the ground floor is the smoking-room in the front block—the first room on the right after entering. Its walls have large panels which contain old paintings of Italian scenes, many of them architectural. The furniture is of the time of Queen Anne, the armchairs covered with green tapestry. Dr. Johnson and James Boswell were frequently entertained in this room on their visit to Scotland.

The modern dining-room and drawing-room are in the back block on the ground floor, extending the whole width of the house, opposite each other, with the long corridor separating them. The outer faces are curved by the shape of the walls, and the inner faces are made to have similar curves, so that two remarkable ovals result. The total length of the two rooms is 80 feet. Folding doors close the rooms, which can be made one great reception-room. They suggest what the entertaining power of a Lord Provost of Edinburgh was in the time of Sir James Dick, the successful merchant.

The tapestry drawing-room has three of its walls covered with Flemish pieces representing Oriental scenes. One has a man's head lying on the floor, so perhaps it is connected with the subject of John the Baptist. Three paintings are of Sir William Dick of Braid, his wife, and his eldest daughter. He was a merchant whose ships traded with many lands. He was Lord Provost of Edinburgh in 1638 and 1639, and his patriotism led him to advance £65,000 to help the Royal Cause. After the Restoration he went to London to try to get some of his money back ; but for his pains he was made bankrupt, thrown into Westminster gaol, and his estates sold at about one-fifth of their value. He died in gaol, and his widow and family were left in poverty.

Sir William's sons scattered, and left his baronetcy unclaimed. Ultimately James Boswell of Auchinleck found the heir in Captain Dick, H.M. Consul at Leghorn, grandson of Sir William's youngest son, and he was duly registered as Sir John Dick, Baronet, of Braid. But he died without male issue, and that baronetcy is definitely extinct.

James Dick who bought Priestfield was a grandson of Sir William

Dick, and doubtless when he received his baronetcy in 1676 there was a nearer heir than he to the older title. His sons died before him, and in 1707 the patent was altered so as to bring the second son of the only surviving daughter into the succession. She was Janet, who married Sir William Cunyngham of Caprington, 2nd Baronet of Lambrughton. Her two sons, therefore, succeeded to baronetcies, and in course of time the two baronetcies have become merged in the successor to the Dick honour. The late baronet was Sir William Stewart Dick-Cunyngham, eleventh holder of the Dick baronetcy of Prestonfield, and ninth of the Lambrughton baronetcy of the Cunynghams. In the Great War he commanded the 10th Battalion of the Black Watch on the Somme and in the Balkans. He had already seen service in Mauritius, Egypt, India, and in the South African War, had many decorations and mentions in dispatches, and did fine work in Edinburgh after the war on behalf of the men who had served. He died in March, 1922, and was succeeded in the baronetcies by his nephew, now Sir Colin Keith Dick-Cunyngham, Baronet.

XL

SALTOUN HALL, PENCAITLAND, EAST LOTHIAN

SALTOUN HALL is the residence of Captain Andrew Mansel
Talbot Fletcher of Saltoun, who bears a name with this terri-
torial connection which has in the last three centuries produced
a number of interesting and capable personages in various depart-
ments of intellectual and social activity. The house is only about
fifteen miles from the Scottish capital, on the road which pursues
its way to the quaint old village of Gifford and then goes on to lose
itself in the Lammermuir Hills in a mere bridle-path between
Penshiel Hill and Herd's Hill. Not far past Pencaitland we cross
the Tyne Water, and see a lodge on our right—white-washed, and
baronial in style. The gateway admits to an avenue about a mile
long through an extensive park, open in the near view, but with woods
in the vista wherever we look afar. At the end of the avenue we see
the Hall with a great open level space in front of it. But on our right
a strong battlemented parapet marks the top of a deep and steep
bank, at the foot of which flows the Saltoun Water.

It is the north front before which we stand, and we look upon a
great pile of masonry. The length of the front is about 180 feet,
of which about 100 feet of the line belong to the great main block,
leaving about 80 feet for a low wing on our left, to the east of the
main block, and standing about 50 feet back from the main line.
The back of the building, which faces the south, is one continuous
line, and the general massiveness of the castle can be appreciated
on this side if we cross the stream so as to take in the picture with
the castle rising high above the bank.

It is hardly possible to say when the present building was begun.
The central tower, so prominent now, is not old. Indeed, there
is nothing in the exterior to suggest antiquity, as it is in that Gothic
domestic architecture which in Scotland is Jacobean. But on the
south front, at the west end, there is a part which is very old ; and
that is undoubtedly where the ancient castle, a real stronghold,
stood for defence on the Saltoun Water.

In the twelfth century and in the first half of the thirteenth
century the manor belonged to the De Morvilles, of whom one was
Lord High Constable of Scotland; but about the year 1260 the

greater part of the lands was in the hands of Sir William de Abernethy. The name is said to be derived from Nicolas de Soulis, one of the competitors for the Scottish Crown in 1291—Soulis Toun merging into Saltoun. It is rather thin, especially as we find the Abernethys in possession after as well as before the time of Nicolas. One of the Abernethys was created Lord Saltoun, and the ninth lord sold the lands to Sir Andrew Fletcher, a Lord of Session known as Lord Innerpeffer, in 1643.

The north front shows us a very impressive and graceful building, consisting, in the main block, of three storeys with a square tower at each end of the line, a great square tower rising from the centre of the building, an arcaded entrance of three wide flattened arches, battlemented parapets, and the usual type of square-headed windows with top mouldings, characteristic of the Gothic. The wing to the east has the same features, and a round tower rises in the recessed angle.

The west end, overhanging the stream, is broad, and looks high. It is not all in one straight line, but bends in an obtuse angle in conformity with the bend of the bank, and at the bend has a round tower on its own foundation. At the south-west angle is a bartizan turret on lines of corbelling. The south front is almost one continuous line, the break being near the west end, where the old block is. A square tower stands out here, with a wide Gothic doorway from which steps descend to the path. An octagonal tower in the line, and further to the east a wide bay of three sides of an octagon, are the only important breaks in an otherwise plain line.

From the arcaded entrance of the north front we proceed into a square hall, beyond which is the saloon, the floor forming a great rectangle. This space was formerly the courtyard of the old castle; now the central tower rises above it with the interior forming a "well." On the west and east sides are galleries on the first floor, with fronts of carved wood in the battlemented designs of the house. A circular gallery round the top floor, and elaborate groined ceilings, are impressive points in the scheme.

At the east end are the stairs which give access to the other floors; and by this end of the main block we approach the long corridor, which runs the whole length of the east extension and is lighted by the whole series of great Gothic windows on the ground floor. It has a very fine groined ceiling, is decorated with Dresden china, and on a white panel set in the wall is this inscription: "This Library was built A.D. 1775 by Andrew Fletcher of Salton to contain that excellent collection of books made by his great-uncle of illustrious memory whose name he bore; Lieut.-Gen. Henry Fletcher

SALTOUN HALL
FROM THE SOUTH-WEST

SALTOUN HALL
THE NORTH FRONT

of Salton inscribes this marble to the memory of his lamented brother : desires to remind their common successors that the love of letters or of arms has always distinguished the family of Salton."

On the other side of the wall which bears this slab is the actual library, of the same length as the corridor except for a small part cut off at the east end to form a smoking-room. The library has a fine oak ceiling, and the bookcases which line the walls are in the typical Gothic style. At one time the oak was covered with a yellow varnish, but that has been removed and now the oak appears in its full beauty.

Above the cases are, at intervals, examples of wood medallions of carved heads, the earliest in existence. They were originally in Stirling Castle, and were given in 1827 to Lady Charlotte Fletcher by General Graham, Governor of the Castle.

The dining-room lies to the west of the saloon, and is full of family portraits. Sir Andrew Fletcher, Lord Innerpeffer the judge, was a son of Robert Fletcher of Innerpeffer and Beuclo in Forfarshire, a burgess of Dundee, and doubtless a successful merchant there. Lord Innerpeffer died in 1650. He was fined £5,000 by Cromwell in 1648. He voted against abandoning Charles I. to the English army, and in 1649 was removed from his offices of judge and commissioner of exchequer because of his adherence to the "Engagement," to which the previous year he had subscribed £8,500 Scots. This was repaid to his son Sir Robert in 1662.

Sir Robert does not seem to have earned any special distinction ; but the third Fletcher of Saltoun, Sir Robert's son, is the Fletcher of whom everyone thinks when " Fletcher of Saltoun " is mentioned. He was Sir Andrew, commonly known as "The Patriot," born in 1653. In 1664 his father, dying, placed him under the care of Gilbert Burnet, then minister designate of the parish of Saltoun. His guardian described him in his *History* as " a Scotch gentleman of great parts and many virtues, but a most violent Republican and extremely passionate." A writer, Macky, is quoted in the *Dictionary of Biography* as giving him " a stern, sour look." But a beautifully clear painting of him which hangs in the dining-room does not bear this out; rather it gives him a pleasant look, which accords with his flowing wig and handsome cravat.

All accounts of him agree that he was a man of absolute truthfulness and honesty, with an absorbing love of freedom and hatred of time-servers. He was a greater terror to his friends than to his opponents, and was against the government of the Duke of Lauderdale, with the result that he had to take refuge in Holland, where he got mixed up with Monmouth's expedition. His shooting of

Dare over a dispute about a horse led to his leaving Monmouth's cause. He went to Spain, fought in Hungary against the Turks, and returned to Scotland with William of Orange. He was strongly against the union of the Parliaments, wrote a good deal, took an active interest in many causes, and died in London in 1716—a brilliant, turbulent man. He never married—perhaps he did not have time; or was it because of that love of freedom? At any rate, the fact saved some good lady from a variety of unpleasant thrills.

His brother Henry acted as tenant of the lands and house, and is absolutely overshadowed by his truly remarkable wife, a daughter of Sir David Carnegie of Pitarrow. She organised industry, established in Saltoun village mills for grinding barley and for making holland cloth, and gave an impetus to manufactures which was felt throughout Scotland.

XLI

SORN CASTLE, MAUCHLINE, AYRSHIRE

SORN CASTLE is in the valley of the River Ayr, a few miles east of the famous town of Mauchline, and in a district where the valley narrows so that it rapidly becomes a glen. A charming avenue leads up to the house on its north front, while the south and west fronts overlook the river, with a most picturesque rustic walk running beside it.

The first view of the house makes a double appeal—comfort and beauty. It looks as if it might have been built quite recently, which is a testimony to the judgment and art with which later additions have been made to a house which has a long history behind it. The handsome porch stands on round columns carrying a heavy canopy, giving three very wide passages with flat arches. The battlemented parapet has the merlons very wide and the crenelles or embrasures very narrow—a modern variation of the ancient form.

The building covers a rectangle, the entrance-front being almost north, and comprising mainly three parts, with an extension of little height to the east. The low extension is the latest part of the whole, but sloping down behind it to the south are low buildings with crow-stepped gables and other evidences of age. They were probably at one time detached. The general features of the north front are a central part with a crow-stepped gable above the parapet, and a very nice oriel window in the wall above the porch, the effect being a suggestion of an old square tower with capehouse, modified. Left and right are wider and lower parts, of which that on the right has a very similar character, while that on the left has three dormer windows instead of the crow-stepped gable of the right.

The other fronts share the leading characteristics which belong to the north front—beautiful corbelling, crow-stepped gables, and battlemented parapets. But the south front displays a special variation in a very solid and prominent balcony with three front arches and an arch at each end, open except that they are guarded by bars, as they overhang the river. A supporting wall is built on the solid rock below, and the balcony is covered by a canopy with a classical parapet. The position is in front of the dining-room.

161   M

The numerous alterations in this wall from its original aspect can be realised from a position actually in the bed of the river just below the dam. On the roof the various superstructures are seen as they probably were in the fifteenth and sixteenth centuries, with the dormer window and the crow-steps. There is the battlement and its gun-shaped gargoyles. I am doubtful about the gargoyles, for an old print which I have, dated 1791, shows openings for drainage instead. At the same time, prints are never entirely reliable for details.

The ages of the different parts are very largely a matter of conjecture. In the castle wall is a tablet claiming that the castle was built in 1409, which may be accepted as true for the original small and strong keep, represented by the part including the angle formed by the west and south fronts. To that was added a part which can be recognised by the difference of the floor levels along the south line. Probably this was done about the end of the fifteenth century, a beautiful corbelling being at the same time placed round the top to carry a parapet. The next great alteration seems to have been made between 1795 and 1805, and to have included the present entrance-front; and the last great restoration or addition was in the sixties of last century.

The date 1409 is quite the latest date for the earliest part, and it is more than probable that there was a house on the site before then. The name " Sorn " is very old, if we accept that it is the Gaelic for a " snout " and that it was applied to a projecting or hummocky surface—for proof of which there are many examples : a Sorne in Mull, another in Morvern, near Loch Sunart, besides others. The lands belonged to the Keiths of Galston, and passed through an heiress, Janet de Keith, to her son Andrew by her first marriage to Sir David de Hamyltoune, of Cadzow. The charter by which she granted the lands was confirmed under the Great Seal in 1406; and the Hamiltons continued owners until an heiress carried the estate into the family of Seton in the reign of James VI. The second Earl of Winton sold the lands to the Loudoun family about 1630. The Earl of Loudoun sold them to William Tennant in 1782; and later owners were the Grahams of Limekilns, Stevensons of Dalgain, and Somervells, before T. W. McIntyre, father of the present laird, bought the estate in 1908.

One of the most interesting personages connected with the castle was the Countess of Loudoun, who lived there fifty years from her widowhood, from 1727 till 1777, when she died within a few months of completing her hundredth year. She did a great deal for the improvement of the parish in many ways. She took gardening and

SORN CASTLE
FROM THE SOUTH-WEST

SORN CASTLE
THE ENTRANCE FRONT

farming into her own hands, and set an example to other landowners in tree-planting, road-making, and the reclaiming of moorland. Much of the beauty of the neighbourhood, now abounding with trees, is due to her influence.

The interior of the house interests both by internal decoration and by the survival of old features. The porch leads into a small entrance-hall which in turn admits to a very fine inner hall occupying the whole centre of the house and including a part of the old baronial hall. At the east end a stair rises to the floor above; and on the north side is a great old fireplace with modifications which retain the old character—it is probably one of the fireplaces of the baronial hall. Oak beams run east to west in the ceiling.

The drawing-room is entered from the inner hall by a door on the right not far from the main entrance. It occupies the north-west corner of the entrance-front, and is lighted by a handsome bow window in the west wall. Two important rooms are on the south front—the study and the dining-room. The study is certainly in the very old part of the house and has a fine oak ceiling, which was treated in the bad old ways of the bad old days of taste—that is, it was plastered over, and not done artistically. The late Mr. McIntyre had the plaster removed, and displayed the beautiful old oak again to view. The principal features of the dining-room are an oak ceiling with white plates and its opening on the artistic arcade which overlooks the river.

It is recorded that King James VI. had a very unpleasant journey to Sorn Castle. The 1st Earl of Winton was a great friend of the King, and when the Earl's only daughter Isobel married James, 1st Earl of Perth, the King honoured the ceremony at Sorn with his presence. He rode from Glasgow over the moor in the middle of winter, and his journey has left two memorials by the way. One is about half-way between Glasgow and Sorn, where he stopped to drink at a well which is still known as the "King's Well"; and the other is not far from that, and is known as the "King's Stable." The name commemorates a jest of the King under adverse circumstances, for his horse sank in the bog, and it was with some difficulty that the King was relieved from his plight. He made the joke that his horse was stabled now, which I suppose means that the horse sank completely. At any rate, the jest gave a name to the place.

An interesting historical fact is that Sorn Castle was held by troops in the days of Charles II. under an old ordinance. The purpose of the garrison was to overawe the Covenanters and to prevent the holding of Conventicles, the governor of the castle being Lieutenant Lewis Lauder. It is said that the troop of dragoons quartered there killed two lads in high-handed fashion, one at Tinkhornhill and the other at Tarbolton. The " curate " is charged by tradition with instigating the latter deed. Probably he was innocent; but in any case he was " rabbled " in 1689 and died the following year.

Alexander Peden, famous among covenanters, was born in the parish of Sorn and returned there to die. He is credited by legend with many prophecies; but Wodrow, the historian of his side, expressed the belief that most of them had been fathered on him.

The present laird of Sorn is J. G. McIntyre.

XLII

THE GRANGE, EDINBURGH

THE Grange House, Grange Loan, Edinburgh, is in these days well within the boundaries of the city, but that is because the city has grown out to it and around it, forming a very attractive residential district. When The Grange House began its life the neighbourhood was by no means alluring, as it formed part of the famous " Burgh Muir." Most people who have even a passing knowledge of Edinburgh know the fine open space on the south side which bears the name of " The Meadows." In days gone by, those " meadows " were under a loch about three-quarters of a mile from east to west and half a mile from north to south, the ground surrounding it, part of the ancient great forest of Drumsheugh, being the " Burgh Muir " and extending from the crags of Arthur's Seat to the village of Dalry on the west, and to the Braid Hills on the south.

That great moor was the place where King James IV. assembled the army which met disaster at Flodden. It was in time of peace the harbourage of broken men who preyed upon travellers ; and in time of pestilence the diseased of the city were driven into it, to be cared for by a chapel which came into existence. Sometimes malefactors were hanged there; and the hanging of six English pirates there in 1554 only cost four shillings—a very cheap job, according to the value of " a shilling Scots " as compared with " a shilling sterling." Across the moor there was a path or road with which the present Grange Loan corresponds, and it was by the side of this road that The Grange House arose.

Its origin is associated with the Church of St. Giles in Edinburgh, the church now known as St. Giles's Cathedral, which only became a cathedral when Charles I. created the See of Edinburgh in order that he might make the excellent William Forbes its bishop. St. Giles, whose Latin name is Egidius, died on September 1, 721, and was taken as the patron saint of lepers, cripples, and beggars. It was the Scottish Matilda, Queen of Henry I. of England, who founded the hospital which gave rise to the parish of St. Giles's, Cripplegate, about the year 1117; and her brother, the Scottish Alexander I., had built a new parish church in Edinburgh to

165

St. Giles in 1112, the old one said to date from the year 854. David I., another brother, conferred the Grange of St. Giles upon the monks of Holme Cultrane, otherwise known as Harehope, an abbey in Cumberland. It need not be surprising that an Edinburgh endowment should be given to a Cumberland abbey, for Cumberland was a possession of the Scottish king.

This gives an approximate date for the beginning of The Grange House, which does not seem to have been occupied by the monks, but by a priest who was their vassal, and thus Vicar of St. Giles's. Maidment states that in 1153 The Grange belonged to the perpetual Vicar of St. Giles's. In any case, it was Church enterprise which developed the wild and waste lands of the moor and gave them a commercial value.

In 1355 David II. resumed possession of the lands, and Robert II. gave his rights in them to his son, who in 1390, as King Robert III., disponed them to one of the family of Wardlaw. The Wardlaws resigned them into the hands of the King in 1506, and James IV. then gave them to John Cant, a burgess of Edinburgh, and his wife. From the Cants they went by sale to William Dick in 1631. In 1755 Isobel Dick, wife of Sir Andrew Lauder of Fountainhall, succeeded through failure of heirs male; and on her death her son Andrew succeeded as Laird of Grange. In 1769 he succeeded his father as baronet of Fountainhall, and took as his name Lauder-Dick. When his son Thomas succeeded, he adopted the style of Sir Thomas Dick-Lauder, 7th Baronet of Fountainhall and 5th Baron of Grange.

The Grange of St. Giles was never a large house, and a print of the year 1700 shows it as a small keep, with an extension on the L plan. It is now swallowed up in the additions which were made in the first half of the nineteenth century. One authority on architecture assumes the date of the castle as 1592, because of a dated doorway which has above it the inscription in capitals—REPOSE ALLEURS, ANNO 1592. It is now within the house, but was then the principal entrance, and as likely as not merely marks the date of the addition to the old keep.

Nearly everything in the neighbourhood seems to have " Grange " in its name. The grounds of the Grange Cricket Club are to the west, separated only by the " Lover's Loan," an old and historical lane. A lodge and arch admit to a short avenue, which has such a curve that at either end it looks long. On the left of the curve is a high bank and the "Monk's Walk." The north front which we approach has a high massive stone archway, with the date 1613 on it; while opposite the house are the griffin columns which indicate an old gateway. The griffins stand on the columns, over-

THE GRANGE
FROM THE SOUTH-WEST

THE GRANGE
THE NORTH FRONT

grown with foliage so that they often have passed unnoticed. They mark the fact that at one time, before the lands were " feued " for the building of the district called " The Grange " there was a north avenue.

It is evident that the north front has been the entrance at least since 1592, as it is still. Probably its only alteration in 1592 was the addition of the octagonal turret at the north-west angle—that is, on the right of the north front. The archway in the north wall enters a courtyard, with the east front of the house on our right. The general character of the north front is that of two gabled ends of east and west blocks, crow-stepped, with a recessed front between them, the gabled ends four storeys and the recessed part three, with dormer windows additional. The east gable-end is of date 1827, which is on the large panel above the doorway in that end, also containing the arms of the families of Dick-Lauder and Cumin. The wide gateway to the left, which has the date 1613, has above it the impaled escutcheons of John Cant and Catherine Creich, his wife. The west gable is old. Between the 1613 gateway and the 1827 doorway is another doorway into the courtyard, with a stone built into the wall above and containing the inscription " 16 W.D. 74," probably the initials of William Dick.

The reconstruction of the house is very fully seen on the south front, where the old fortalice can be fully identified, approximately in the middle of the view. The western part, on the left, is the part which was added to make the L shape. The general features are corner turrets, crow-stepped gable, angle tower, and a large bay window thrown out in the crow-stepped east part of the line. The old east front is completely covered by additions, which are carried round on the south front to cover half of the wall of the old keep, so that what is visible of the old keep is the south-west angle, with the parts of the walls containing it which are bounded by round towers.

The door on the north front admits to a small hall and a passage which runs to the back. Across the passage we reach an old vaulted room which stretches to the west, and in the north wall of which is the doorway with the " Repose Alleurs, anno 1592." The porch, which is a small square, contains an oak settle believed with good reason to have been part of the bedstead of Cardinal James Beaton.

The stair rises from the hall and contains a picture of Sir William Dick in prison, visited by his wife, five sons, and two daughters—a strange picture, but true to fact. On the right of the landing the dining-room is entered by a doorway in the wall of the keep, 5 feet thick. In its present state it is an exceedingly handsome room,

45 feet long and 18 broad. A small room to the south of the dining-room occupies the remainder of the old keep on that floor, and was the study of Sir Thomas Dick-Lauder, the 7th Baronet, who wrote so much. In the third storey of the keep is a room called " Queen Mary's Room," but there seems no reason to believe that Queen Mary ever occupied the room or was ever in The Grange.

There is a legend that an underground passage led from The Grange of St. Giles to the Church of St. Giles. The passage did exist and was, no doubt, a safe refuge, but it is hardly likely that it extended so far.

William Dick and his wife Anne Seton, with her sisters, entertained Prince Charles Edward at The Grange in 1745, and the Prince is said to have danced with the ladies. The youngest of the sisters, according to the story, presented him with a white rose, whereupon he took the thistle from his bonnet and presented it to the lady.

And there are literary associations, chiefly connected with Sir Thomas. Sir Walter Scott and he were on intimate terms, and Sir Walter is said to have visited The Grange; but that is unfounded. Lord Cockburn was a frequent visitor, and was among the last who saw Sir Thomas.

The present laird is Sir George Dick-Lauder, the 10th Baronet, and a grandson of the literary baronet who gave The Grange House its present charming form.

XLIII

THE INCH, LIBERTON, MIDLOTHIAN

THE Inch, Liberton, in the County of Midlothian, is the property of Brigadier-General Sir Robert G. Gilmour, Baronet, C.B., C.V.O., D.S.O., of Liberton and Craigmillar. It stands in one of the most romantic parts of the country surrounding the capital. The writer of a notice of the parish of Liberton which appeared in the *Transactions* of the Society of Antiquaries of Scotland in 1792 gave the origin of the name as "Lepertown," but stated that there was no tradition of a hospital.

The site of The Inch was an island in ancient days, *inch* being the same word as the Irish *innis*, and meaning an island. Up to 1760 the floods surrounding the house were an inconvenience, and at an earlier date entrance was obtained by a drawbridge. The writer of the notice, who was the parish minister at the time, gives the date of the building of the house as 1617, with the addition of a two-storeyed part at the north-west in 1634, and the buildings to the north later. He further described the mansion as having been built by the family of Winram, and the gablets of three dormer windows facing the court as bearing the following letters: north, I.W.; south, I.S.; and centre, I.W.S., with date 1634. The initials I.W. stand for James Winram, I.S. for his wife Jean Swinton, and the three letters are a combination of both. Both names have been mentioned in charters under the Great Seal of Scotland. The Inch and Craigmillar have been Gilmour property since 1660; Upper Liberton has been a Little property since 1522.

The date 1617 is not early enough for the whole house. There is a part which has that date over the old entrance, now in the inside of the house. But there are two rooms on the ground floor which are marked by their structure as much older, for they have barrel-vaulted roofs and very thick walls. The larger of the two, now used as a dining-room, bears a remarkable resemblance to the Crypt in Glamis Castle, although the Crypt is about double the size of the other. The year 1522 is not too early a date for these two rooms of The Inch, and probably that part existed before 1500.

The present ground plan is much like a capital **E** without the middle line, and that is the result of growth. The south front is about 105 feet long, and contains the oldest and most important parts. The east front is about 10 feet longer; and the entrance is in the south front. The north front is not so high as the south, and forms practically a second house. A battlemented wall fills up the west side and completes the enclosing of a courtyard.

The part on the right of the south front is the oldest, now three full storeys in height and possessing a row of dormer windows. At the other end of the line, our left, is a part about 100 years old, originally lower by one storey than that on the right. The present laird raised it to a height practically equal to the other, and at the same time built a narrow part between the two to contain the modern porch. This narrow part encloses in the new hall a most interesting bit of the old exterior, which has been kept carefully exposed to view.

The new part of the south front is very distinct, partly by its design and partly by its dressed stonework, the rest of that front being harled, and the same distinction being observed between the century-old wall and the new dormers above it. That new part merges naturally into the west end of the block, which has been modified under the same scheme. Dormer windows, crow-stepped gablets, turrets and windows projected on corbels—all these appear in the usual combination of an old Scottish house. Extending west of the battlemented wall is a larger open courtyard, from which a general understanding of the build of the house can be realised, and in the south-east corner of which was the ancient entrance. There are dormer windows facing the courtyard with the date 1636 carved on them. Over the old entrance approached from this side is the date 1617 in the partly concealed pediment now within the house. These dates, with what has already been written, give us four periods of construction—1617, 1636, 1807, and 1892; and they are only additions to a building already there.

The house and grounds lie between two roads which lead into Edinburgh, and an avenue approaches from a lodge on each road. The older is the old Dalkeith road which passes through "Little France," where the ladies of the Scottish Courts spent many pleasant days.

A striking object to the east of the house is a tall sundial standing in a place which is closely surrounded by thick and well-trimmed yew hedges. It has four old faces, much worn, with a base and pedestal which are new. Monograms of J.G., M.G., and R.G., with heraldic figures, accompany the date 1660.

The entrance-hall on the south front has on the right a part of the old outer wall. Built into it is a large panel with the Royal Arms

THE INCH
THE EAST FRONT
AND THE SUNDIAL

THE INCH
AN OLD VAULTED ROOM

of Scotland and the initials I.Q., which stand for Jacobus Quartus—James IV. There are stones from the old Bridge-end House at Craigmillar Castle and from Canonmills House, both possessions of the Gilmours. Darnley's thick buff coat and gloves are there, and a sword of Cromwell, which has on it : " Belonged to Oliver Cromwell, Lord Protector. Naseby Battle, June 14, 1645. Dunbar Battle, September 3, 1650. Praise to the Lord of Hosts." These came from Craigmillar Castle, which Cromwell captured.

The barrel-vaulted room, now a dining-room, is the kind of room which good Americans would like to take down and rebuild " at home." It is 40 feet by 25 feet, lighted by windows in the east and the south, those on the side showing the thickness of the walls. The arching is comparatively flat and is not plastered over. The room adjoining it can be entered from it and is of the same character. The position of these rooms and their character all testify to great age, supported by the evidence of a corner of the larger room, where a " wheel-stair " in the old outside wall leads up to the room above by a trap-door in the floor.

Many of the rooms throughout the house are very quaint—the " crimson room," with its four-poster bed and hangings at least 250 years old ; the "yellow room" just beside it, with a collection of prints of men who were " out in the 'fifteen "; the " king's room " with an original " powder closet "; and the " buff room," which has a shutter-board window, very difficult to describe in words, but so unique that I do not know of another house which has one.

It is quite clear that the lands were at one time the property of the monks of Holyrood Abbey. The Winrams are the first owners known after the Reformation, and it is remarkable that one of them was sub-prior of St. Andrews at the beginning of the Reformation, and a " Superintendent " afterwards. George Winram, of Liberton, was the owner in 1644; and his son, Colonel Winram, was Lieutenant-Governor of Edinburgh Castle under the Duke of Gordon in the siege of 1688-1689. The Inch, Craigmillar, and Nether Liberton, belonged to Sir John Gilmour in 1660. From that year until 1774, the County of Edinburgh was represented in Parliament by the Gilmour family—namely, Sir John, Sir Alexander, Sir Charles, and Sir Alexander—except for very short intervals.

The present laird is a Gordon by birth, and his father was a Worlige, who took the name of Gordon when he married Anne, daughter of Robert Gordon of Hallhead and Esslemont. Robert Gordon had married Jane Little-Gilmour, through whom the present laird entered into the inheritance of the Littles and the

Gilmours on the death of his great-uncle Walter James Little-Gilmour in 1887.

The last of the Gilmours of Craigmillar was Sir Alexander, an officer of the regiment which is now the Grenadier Guards. He was wounded and taken prisoner at St. Cas in 1758. He was the third baronet of his line, and was succeeded in the estate by William Charles Little of Liberton, the grandson of his father's sister Helen. Of the Littles, three stand out prominently in the early days, the first being Clement, who bought Upper Liberton in 1522. His son Clement founded the library of Edinburgh University, and had the distinction of being proclaimed at the Market Cross of Edinburgh as a rebel against Queen Mary. He was followed by his brother William, who was Provost of Edinburgh and a favourite of King James VI. He distinguished himself by burning down Restalrig Tower in the absence of its doughty and quarrelsome owner, Logan of Restalrig—a feat which was so inconvenient to the King that the latter would not for a long time pass through the gates of Edinburgh on his way to Holyroodhouse. Lauder of Fountainhall wrote a very lively account of the incident.

XLIV

THIRLESTANE CASTLE, LAUDER, BERWICKSHIRE

THIRLESTANE CASTLE is the seat of one of the oldest and most notable Scottish families, the Maitlands ; and the district in which the castle is situated gives the title of the head of the family, who is the Earl of Lauderdale. Lauderdale is the valley of the River Leader, which rises on the southern slopes of the Lammermuir Hills and flows in a rapidly widening valley until it joins the River Tweed. The castle stands on a bank which overhangs the River Leader. There are the ruins of an older Thirlestane Castle two miles directly to the east of the present building. It is on the Brunta Burn, and developed from the usual type of square keep into a very great stronghold.

The period of King David I. of Scotland brings us into contact with the present Thirlestane—that is, early in the twelfth century. There was an old fort known as Lauder Fort, which accounts say is embodied in the present Thirlestane. Some say that Lauder Fort was built by the English in the reign of David I., which means between 1124 and 1153. Another account says that it was the English Edward I. who built it, which puts it a century and a half later ; and this is quite likely, for Edward I. had conquered Scotland and was building forts to hold his conquest. The most striking point is that, however early we may put the date, the family of Maitland was already there. One of them is named Sir Richard de Mautland, which perhaps gives a clue to the derivation of the name.

The long avenue reaches the castle from the north, and the principal front faces the west, with a very great length from north to south. It presents a great variety of outline. A terrace with tennis courts extends in front of it, a wall supporting the terrace on the west side and raising it a few feet above the park, which spreads out in a great level expanse. The general form of the building now is that of a capital T; and as we look at the main west front we must think of the T as being upside down—the west front is the crossing line. That front contains a central block of an unusual and very beautiful symmetrical form. The middle of it is a great square

173

tower with an ogee roof. On each side is a lower tower, projected much in front of the line of the middle tower and slightly overlapping its sides. These side towers have round high bartizans at the outside angles, surmounted by conical roofs. Their inner sides have balustraded balconies connecting them across the middle tower above the first and third storeys. The entrance doorway is below the lower balcony and so in a recess. The side towers are rounded, but were squared off completely at the top above the higher balcony, and on their further sides below the start of the bartizans, when still lower square blocks were added with a further advance of the line, one block on each side. This leads to a very unusual feature : the entrance is not on the ground floor, but on the first floor, and on this level the whole of the enclosed space forms a paved terrace to which a straight stair of about twenty steps leads up. The ground floor is put forward under the pavement and contains several rooms, while a very charming classical balustrade fronts the pavement. The character of the balustrade is repeated in the balconies and the parapets of the main side towers.

The further wings are much varied, parts projected, others recessed, some windows thrown out on corbels with an oriel character, windows on the roof line having ornamental pediments, and some of the roofs having the ogee form. Altogether it is a unique frontage. On account of the T shape there are many frontages. The upright line of the T gives a north front and a south front, which have, generally speaking, the same architectural forms as each other. Taken as a block, this part has a great round tower at each angle of the oblong—that is, four in all. Two of them have been described as the squared off towers of the main front, and the other two are similar, with modifications. But along the sides there is a wealth of architectural beauty. A gallery runs along the front of the fourth storey on each side, north and south. On the north side the gallery runs on a combination of arches and corbels ; on the south side it is carried on arches. On both sides there is a middle round tower squared at the gallery level, while on each frontage there is a slender round tower on each side of the middle tower and supporting the galleries, the galleries having classical balustrades.

There are three leading dates in the evolution of this truly magnificent castle—1595, 1675, and 1841. The first is given as the date of building a castle on the site of the old Lauder Fort, two years after the death of the first Lord Maitland of Thirlestane, and in the time of the 1st Earl of Lauderdale, whose father and grandfather had in turn been Lord Chancellors of Scotland. The second date marks the extension of the west front by the addition

THIRLESTANE CASTLE
THE CENTRE OF THE GREAT WEST FRONT

THIRLESTANE CASTLE
THE NORTH FRONT

of the first wings. And the third date brings the buildings to their present aspect.

As to the interior, originally the great oblong with north and south faces was the castle, the entrance being where it is now, which was only a west end. There were four rooms on each floor, one room entered from another, communication being also obtained by many stairs.

Entering from the paved terrace, we are in a square hall. On the left is a passage from which rises the grand staircase to the drawing-room floor, where the ante-drawing room is over the entrance-hall. The drawing-room is in the old block, with windows looking out to north and south, and the walls here are 10 feet thick. There are numerous beautiful ceilings, of which some were done by George Dunsterfeldt and Mathias Jansen, whom the Duke of Lauderdale brought from Holland in 1675. They are said to have taken five years to do the work, which cost the Duke £1,500—a very large sum in that day. In the artistic and decorative work it is believed that Robert Mylne, the King's Master Mason, and Sir William Bruce, both had a considerable share. In the various rooms are paintings of historical persons done by Sir Peter Lely, Romney, Raeburn, Reynolds, Gainsborough, Sir Thomas Lawrence, Hoppner, and others.

The laird with whom begins the modern history of the family was Sir Richard Maitland, the 12th Laird of Thirlestane, known also by his judicial title of Lord Lethington. His eldest son William is the famous " Secretary Lethington." The brother of the Secretary was Sir John, who in 1587 was Chancellor of Scotland. He was created Baron Maitland of Thirlestane in 1590 and died in 1593. The senior line died out in the person of James, son of Maitland of Lethington, who sold Lethington to his uncle John ; and it is the line of that John which is the historic Lauderdale family. His son, also John, was the 1st Earl of Lauderdale.

The character of Secretary Lethington has been so much disputed that it is difficult to arrive at a true estimate. He was so moderate in his views in both religion and politics, so much mixed up in those days, that he was considered disloyal to friends and partial to enemies. He tried to moderate the violence of John Knox to Queen Mary, and to reconcile the Queen to the religion of her people ; and he failed in both directions. It was only then that he joined Kirkaldy of Grange, the Queen's man, in Edinburgh Castle, in 1571. When the castle was captured he was condemned to death, but died in prison at Leith, some said by poison self-administered.

The Secretary's brother John was with him in Edinburgh

Castle and was sent a prisoner to Tantallon Castle, and did not obtain full liberty until the resignation of the Regent Morton; and then he threw himself heartily into the movement for the complete ruin of his enemy. He became Lord Chancellor of Scotland.

The only Duke, created in 1672, died in 1682. He was in the early days of the trouble with Charles I. a Covenanter; but after the surrender of the King by the Scottish army to Cromwell he became a party to " The Engagement," by which Charles was to accept the Covenant; and from that time he never wavered from the loyalty which was a tradition of the family.

He was succeeded by his brother Charles as 3rd Earl of Lauderdale; and it is from this Earl that the present holder of the titles is descended.

XLV

TRAQUAIR HOUSE, INNERLEITHEN, PEEBLES-SHIRE

THERE is much history attaching to Traquair House, which is one of the very few Scottish houses continuously inhabited since the twelfth century. It is often said to be the oldest house in Scotland which can claim uninterrupted occupation since it was built. But I know that this claim is also made for other houses, among them Dunrobin Castle; and I know that Dunrobin Castle has been continuously occupied since its foundation, which was just about the same date as Traquair. Traquair has received much less alteration and addition than Dunrobin, and therefore presents a more realistic picture of the kind of house in which the great ones of past centuries lived.

It is in the County of Peebles, which is a most beautiful part of the Lowlands of Scotland. Innerleithen is about a mile distant from the house. The River Tweed flows through the grounds, and at one time ran so close under the walls that the Laird was able to fish from his windows. There was a certain amount of occasional discomfort in this nearness of the river, when it came down in flood and almost surrounded the house. So one of the owners diverted the river and turned it about a quarter of a mile from its old course, and all that remains of the old course near the house is a backwater densely wooded, supremely beautiful, and a sanctuary of water-fowl.

The front of the house faces the south-west and is approached by a long avenue fully wooded. At a distance of a furlong or more the avenue crosses the River Quair, a very pretty stream of fair dimensions, giving the name to the house and the village. The name is said to mean " the hamlet on the winding river," a meaning quite describing the character of the stream, which rises in the neighbourhood of three summits—Slake Law, Dun Rig, and White-knowe Head, away to the south-west. The hills named rise respectively to the height of 2,229, 2,433, and 1,676 feet—respectable little mountains. The birches in the valley of the Quair are the remains of what was at one time the great Ettrick Forest. A clump near the village is generally accepted as the inspiration of Crawford's ballad, " The Bush aboon Traquair."

No definite date can be assigned for the building of the earliest part of the house, but it may be conjectured from certain facts. In the opening of its story it was a royal residence, and it was here that William the Lion, between the years 1175 and 1178, granted a charter which made the hamlet of Glasgow, now a city of over a million inhabitants, a Bishop's Burgh. That fact makes Traquair House at least 750 years old.

As we approach the house we find a great grassy quadrangle facing us, the avenue dividing in front of it and the water on our left. To the right extend the fields of the demesne. Next we see a fine gateway with sideposts of rustic stone-work and a low wall on each side carrying an iron railing. Each of the posts, and lower posts of a like kind which support the railing, are surmounted by classical vases. A charming piece of ornamental ironwork extends between the sideposts above the iron gate, and has a coat of arms surmounted by a coronet occupying the centre.

The wall and gateway form the south-west side of a rectangle which is the fore-court so typical of old Scottish houses. Opposite us is the tall mass of the house, and the other sides are low buildings, which are additions belonging to the period of King Charles I. The gateway is said to have suggested to Sir Walter Scott his picture of Tullyveolan in *Waverley*, and this is more than probable, as we are in what is commonly called " the Scott country."

At first the mansion was only a single tower, placed on a sharp bend of the Tweed. That part is to be seen now as the half to our left when we look at the front. There is little on the outside to attest its age, for the stonework is covered with roughcast plaster, and the regularly placed small windows are probably enlargements. The small square bartizan on the outside end of the wall need not be a part of the early building, although its rough shape indicates that it is old. It is only roughly speaking the left half of the whole building, for it is approximately 50 feet long as against 40 feet for the other part. A slight curve in the ridge of the roof marks a point at which an extension was made to the right; but this was not the first extension, and the limit of the original tower is probably marked between the second and third dormer windows from the left. And then a new front was added on the right.

This new front has a round bartizan on the left, and a round tower rising from the foundations on the right, both with interesting corbelling. All these features, with the low extensions forming opposite sides of the fore-court, give the whole house a remarkably quaint appearance.

Few houses have had so little interference with the original

TRAQUAIR HOUSE
THE FRONT,
FROM THE SOUTH-WEST

TRAQUAIR HOUSE
THE BACK OF THE HOUSE
FROM THE SOUTH-EAST

interior ; and that interior is full of interest. A passage runs along the low part on the right and turns into the second oldest part. On the floor above is a room made noteworthy by its association with Mary Queen of Scots. It is in the oldest part, approached by a passage through the second oldest part. A window which looks out to the front on the left of the porch lights the stair ; and then we reach Queen Mary's room, which has one window to the front and two to the back. Its present appearance is that of a sitting-room, in which two doors next to each other have a special interest. One is the entrance to a room used by Darnley, while the other is that of a passage which tradition says was used as the sleeping room of the infant King James VI. Two floors higher up, and directly above Queen Mary's room, is one which contains Queen Mary's bed. The room is one of two which form the library, and the wooden bed is a remarkable example of the taste of the period. This piece of furniture remained in a lumber room for an indefinable time, and there is no doubt about its genuineness, although there is a possibility that the posts supporting the very magnificent canopy are of a later date. The house is full of the most delightful relics of past ages and of the historical people of those ages, stowed away in chests and in odd rooms which seem never to have been modernised at any time.

The back of the house stands high above two terraces, the lower flanked by two small buildings with ogee roofs, forming the terminals of walls at the ends of the house. The back of the house is a single line, with the division between the oldest and the second oldest parts well marked, and a general length of line of about 125 feet.

The place seems to have remained a royal residence until King Robert Bruce gifted the lands to Sir James Douglas. From that family they went through those of Murray, Douglas of Cluny, and the Boyds, until they were resumed by the Crown in 1469. James III. gave them to William Rogers, his physician, much to the disgust of his nobles. Rogers was glad to sell them for a small sum to James Stewart, Earl of Buchan, who bestowed them on his natural son James, who thus became the first of the Stewarts of Traquair. A descendant, Sir John Stuart, was created by Charles I. Lord Stuart of Traqu'r in 1633, and was afterwards made Earl of Traquair. It was he who made the additions and alterations. He was a prominent Minister of the King's wishes, and ended by losing all in the King's Cause, so that at last he lived on the casual gifts of his former friends, and died in abject poverty in 1659. The story of his life is full of dramatic interest.

His son succeeded, and the line was continued until the death in 1861 of Charles, 8th Earl, when the title became dormant. His sister, the Lady Louisa Stuart, inherited the estates, and died in 1875. By the Will of the 8th Lord Traquair they then went to the Honourable Henry Maxwell, of the family of the Earl of Nithsdale, with which the Traquair family had intermarried more than once. Henry Maxwell was a son of the 9th Lord Herries, and added to that of Maxwell the name of Stuart. The present laird, Arthur Maxwell-Stuart, is his son.

XLVI

TYNINGHAME HOUSE, DUNBAR, EAST LOTHIAN

NOT far from the sea stands Tyninghame, in surroundings of romantic beauty, and in a corner of the Lothians which carries us back to the early history of our race. The natural features retain in a less degree than many other parts of the country their old Celtic names, instead of which we find in East Lothian and Berwickshire " wicks " and " tons " and " fords " and " hames," proclaiming the blood of the sea-rovers; while an occasional "craig" testifies to the survival of a Celtic element, preserved by the sea-rovers taking wives of the conquered inhabitants.

Tyninghame is the " home " or settlement on the Tyne, a stream which is not polluted by the baleful influence of numberless factories, and where the gentle angler is often seen striving to lure the still more gentle trout from its element. Tyninghame is a village, and not far from it is Tyninghame House, the residence of the Earl of Haddington. The *Picture of Scotland,* an interesting book published early in the nineteenth century, has the following remark about the house : " Of Tyninghame House itself, some idea may be formed from the curious fact that all the ten successive Earls of Haddington have made a point of *adding a piece to it.*" The grounds extend to the shores of the North Sea, where lofty cliffs form " St. Baldred's Cradle." The name is another evidence of the early civilisation of East Lothian.

St. Baldred founded a church at Tyninghame about the year 600, and by virtue of the church Tyninghame remained a separate parish until it was joined to Whitekirk in 1760. A relic of this old dedication remains in two beautiful Norman arches of an east end apse forming the chancel of what is often called Tyninghame Abbey. Between these arches, in a recessed and pointed arch on the south side, lies a recumbent figure in stone, with three shields carved above. Probably these arches rose soon after the spoiling of the church and village by Aulaf the Dane in 941. The manor and parish were in later times adjuncts of the see of St. Andrews, and were conferred on St. Mary's College when that was erected. The tithes have remained the property of that college, but the lands have belonged to the Earls of Haddington since 1628.

Tyninghame House stands close to these relics, and has not the appearance of age, although it is old. The reason is that it was renovated by Charles, the 8th Earl, in 1791, while in 1829 it was greatly enlarged and made fresh and new in appearance by a facing of red stone. Exactly how old was the old house it is difficult to say ; but there was a house on the lands in 1094, in the days of King Duncan, when it was owned by the Lairds of Bass—the island of the solan geese not far distant. In 1617 Isabella Hepburn, the Lady of the Bass, made additions to it; and in 1628, when the Earl of Haddington received this title in exchange for that of Earl of Melrose, he acquired Tyninghame by purchase. But before the time of the Lady of the Bass it must have received additions under the Bishops of St. Andrews, who used it as a country residence as early as the thirteenth century.

A very long avenue leads from the village, and the first view of the house fills one with admiration of the grand pile. Its irregularity of plan is apparent. On the right is a four-storeyed elevation, topped by a crow-stepped gable. The porch projects in front of this part. On the left of the porch is a lower elevation, with the same number of storeys, the summit being a crow-stepped gable broken at the top into three similar gablets. This part projects further than the other, while from the angle between the two rises a round turret. To the left again is a low frontage projecting still further, and also having a round turret in the angle and the crow-stepped gable. The windows on this side are mostly mullioned and transomed, the middle elevation having a specially handsome window of this kind.

The west front presents the most attractive view of all. It has an almost unbroken line, the one break being near the middle and consisting of a round tower on its own foundation rising a little higher than the rest of the front and having a conical roof above some delicate broken corbelling. Crow-stepped gables and gablets, mullioned and transomed windows, fine bays thrown out from the wall, and pedimented dormer windows, make up the detail of this front. Along the whole of this side extends an elevated architectural terrace with classical balusters, and the terrace is continued round by the south front. A terrace garden lies below the architectural terrace, and from it a flight of steps leads down to a lawn, from the south-west corner of which a delightful view is obtained of the two terraces and the west and south fronts of the house. The south front is broken by the east and west wings forming a courtyard which is artistically tiled. From the entrance to this court rises a handsome stair giving an approach to the encircling terrace and suggesting an English rather than a Scottish house.

TYNINGHAME HOUSE
FROM THE SOUTH-WEST

TYNINGHAME HOUSE
THE BALCONY STEPS

The general arrangement of the interior begins with the outer hall entered from the north front. Beyond it is an inner hall, from which by steps on the right we reach the library on the west front. On this front further south are the ante-drawing-room and the drawing-room extending into the newer part of the house, and having the courtyard of the south front on the east of the drawing-room. The outer hall is decorated with many specimens of arms.

From the ante-room extends east along the south front of the house, looking out on the south courtyard, a really remarkable room called " The Corridor." It is a long room which is lighted from the east front as well as from the south. The east window is of stained glass, the three lower lights containing the arms of the family and of families connected with that of Haddington. It contains many curious articles, among them a beautiful and quaint cabinet given by James VI. There is a reliquary in the form of a crucifix containing a watch. Among the paintings is that of Lady Grizell Baillie, who became Lady Murray, and left an interesting volume of *Memoirs*. She was the elder sister of Rachel, who married Lord Binning, son of the 6th Earl of Haddington. She was the heiress of Jerviswoode, which she left to her sister and her sister's second son. Thus came the name of Baillie into the Haddington family.

In many respects the most interesting feature of "The Corridor" is the wonderful collection of Bibles made by the late Earl. It comprises ninety-five versions of different years, in the English language, beginning with Matthew's, published in 1537.

The library is beautifully lighted by a bay window which looks out upon the terrace. The walls are lined with bookcases three-fourths of the way up, and above that line are family paintings. Among them is that of Thomas, the 6th Earl, in the character of Simon, the Dutch skipper. This Earl has special claims to be remembered, with his wife, who was a sister of the 1st Earl of Hopetoun, on account of their pioneer work in " afforestation." The lady got the idea first, and all the knowing people said it was a mad idea. But her husband thought differently, so they bought out the rights of various people in the " Muir of Tyninghame," a waste piece of land of 300 acres Scots, and planted it with trees. This was in 1707, and the result was a great success—and Binning Wood ! The success led to the planting of a total area of 1,800 acres, many of the trees being oak. Another feature was the planting of holly hedges, which now have a total length of 2,952 yards.

On the left of the inner hall a handsome staircase leads to the upper floors, and on its walls are two fine pieces of tapestry, which have been preserved for the family in a remarkable manner. They had lain long in a lumber-room until, when the late Lord Haddington was clearing out many useless bits of furniture, a joiner told him that there were " some old carpets " there. They turned out to be fine old tapestries which had been left to the family under a condition that they should not be allowed to pass into other hands. The dining-room is close to this stair, in the east part of the north front.

The ancestry of the Haddington family goes back to Gilbert, who received a grant of the lands of Cadzow; and all the Hamiltons appear to be descended from him, although the surname only began with his grandson. The late lord died at an advanced age. His son Lord Binning died before him, so the present Earl, the 12th, is the grandson of the late Earl.

XLVII

WEMYSS CASTLE, EAST WEMYSS, FIFE

WEMYSS CASTLE stands high above the northern shore of the Firth of Forth and is approached by avenues from several directions. It lies almost midway between the towns of Kirkcaldy and Leven, with the principal front facing the north in a line of at least 190 feet. The name is pronounced " Weems," and is said to be derived from the " caves " which are numerous along the shore. The Gaelic for a cave is *uamh*. The south front looks out on the Firth of Forth from the edge of a rocky eminence with gardens below, and is not less in length than the north front. At the east end the width is about 100 feet, and at the west end about 80 feet.

The building as we see it now may be attributed to three periods, marked generally by the dates 1421, 1670, and 1880. But it is probable that the earliest part is a successor of one for which permission was given to Sir John Wemyss of Kincaldrum, Reres, and Wemyss, in 1392. The castle was to be built on his lands of Reres.

The part at the east end is the oldest. In front runs a circular wall containing a courtyard, and as it curves round to the east it encircles the rock while it dips very rapidly to a rough natural terrace. A narrow path follows the wall and ends in a long old flight of steps reminiscent of a postern gate and leading down to the rough terrace. Where the steps begin the wall ends, but the curve is continued by an outwork like a barbican tower, built on the natural terrace, and rising practically to the level of the ground on the north terrace.

The general aspect of the north front is a middle part with large mullioned and transomed windows and an extensive porch, while a large square tower stands at each end. The porch belongs to the year 1880. At the angle made by the junction of the great square block on the left is the clock tower with two interesting features— high up, in a panel, a sculptured head of Mary Queen of Scots, who visited the castle; and the other a doorway, with a passage from it winding round to the east to the original main entrance. The east end is a mighty mass of masonry, plastered roughcast, built upon the rock, and buttressed at the base with rough stonework.

The west end is also varied, but is more recent. The rock slopes down more regularly: steps lead down from the north to an open stretch of lawn; more steps go lower to another level; and then at a distance further steps go down to the sea.

The long south front is by far the most attractive. Passing round from the west square block there is a wide and long paved expanse, with the castle towering above us on the left, and on our right the parapet of a great wall on the top of the cliff. On our left is a series of six high and wide Norman arches, built in front of the castle and forming an arcade. At the east end of the pavement a long flight of steps leads up to a terrace forming the roof of the arcade. From the top of these steps it is possible to get a good view of the east wall of the south front—the very oldest bit of building of the visible castle. Nearly all the valued features of castles of its age are to be seen in this part.

The origin of the house is bound up with the origin of the family of Wemyss. Some hold that they are descended from Macduff, the great Thane of Fife. The *Orygynale Cronykil* of Andrew Wyntoun, who died about 1420, says that a Wemyss was sent with Sir Michael Scot of Balwearie to bring home to Scotland the " Maid of Norway," the girl Queen :

> " To this passage thai ordanyd then
> Honorabil Knychtis, and gret men;
> Duelland in-to Fyfe war twa,
> Thir the namys war of tha;
> Of the Wemys Schir Dawy,
> Schyre Mychel Scot of Balwery."

Sir Michael Wemyss, the father of that ambassador Sir David, was one of the barons who met at Norham in 1291, the year after the death of the young Queen Margaret; he was then a supporter of John Baliol. In 1296 he did homage to Edward I. of England at Stirling and Berwick; and in 1304 Edward stayed a day and a night at the castle. In spite of the homage and the hospitality Edward was distrustful, and sent orders to Sir Aymer de Valence to destroy Sir Michael's property. Sir David succeeded his father ; and a grandson of the second son of Sir David is said to have been the real founder of the family—Sir John Wemyss of Kincaldrum, Reres, and Wemyss. It was he who suggested to Wyntoun to write the *Chronicle*, and his period corresponds with a date over a doorway which is now in the interior.

The generations go on until baronets began in 1625, when Sir John Wemyss became one reluctantly. But his reluctance was

WEMYSS CASTLE
THE NORTH FRONT

WEMYSS CASTLE
THE GREAT DINING-ROOM

rewarded in 1628 by his advancement to be Lord Wemyss of Elcho, followed in 1633 by his being made Earl of Wemyss and Lord Elcho and Methil. David, the 2nd Earl, is notable for the systematic working of the coal measures. He built the fine south front of the castle from the old part to the west square block, and probably the west face as it is now. His daughter and heiress married a Wemyss of Burntisland.

The castle was brought to its present appearance by the grandmother of the present laird, Captain Michael Wemyss, about 1880. She was the widow of James Erskine Wemyss of Wemyss. She filled in the great forecourt on the north side and made a magnificent inner hall. The interior wall tells its own tale, for it is extremely thick. Below the castle on the east side are some wonderfully fine vaulted rooms. In one is kept a silver tray which is said to have been given by the King of Norway to Sir David Wemyss. The carving on the plate is greatly worn, but the date " 1296 " in the centre is very clear.

The interior has some of the finest rooms to be seen in the country, both as regards size and adornment. The great hall is entered from a small hall on the north front. It is the inner hall filling up the old forecourt, and it is about 80 feet long from west to east. It is a good two storeys high, lighted by great mullioned and transomed windows. The south side, the old exterior wall, is solid in the first storey, but pierced in the second by four doubled arches in oblong frames, open so as to light a gallery which extends on the south and east sides. The great staircase rises from the south-east corner of the great hall to the gallery. Near it at its beginning are a door and a short passage which lead to the great dining-hall in the oldest part. Its windows look out to the south through walls 5 feet thick, it has a large stone fireplace, and a magnificent ceiling which is not itself old but is a copy of an old one in another part of the castle. The chief wall decorations are three old tapestries.

Behind the great hall is the " oak room " with interesting paintings in the panels—James VI., Lucy Walters, and Mary Queen of Scots, with the date 1566. The ceiling of the great hall is very fine, and the panelling is a work of art. The hall has many excellent paintings. The gallery enables an impressive view of the hall to be obtained, and is also the means by which many rooms are reached. One of them, the " Montague Room," has a painting of the Lord Elcho who was " out in the 'forty-five." Two other rooms, of which the ceilings have been copied, have in them kings' heads, winged cherubs' heads, flying cherubs, and curious faces—all done by Italian workmen when that part of the castle was built about

1670, and quite different from the work done at Holyroodhouse and Winton by Italian artists at the beginning of that century.

Such a fine old house as this ought, of course, to have a ghost. And it has. Her name is " Green Jean," and she is said to wander all about rather than to concentrate her presence in one part. I trust that she is not the same " Green Jean " whom I know in two other houses, but I fear the worst, as none of them receives proper attention from her.

It is strange that the estate which gives an Earl his title has gone to a junior and untitled branch of the family. The titled family is on the south side of the Forth, with seat at Gosford. The 4th Earl of Wemyss, whose eldest son, Lord Elcho, was attainted and forfeited for the adventure of 1745, made a fresh entail, by which the estates on the south of the Firth were settled on the second son and his line, while the estate of Wemyss was settled on the third son James and his line. The titles went with the line of Francis, the second son.

XLVIII

WHITTINGEHAME HOUSE, PRESTONKIRK, EAST LOTHIAN

WHITTINGEHAME HOUSE is in the parish of Whittinge-hame and in the County of Haddington, or East Lothian ; and the first thing which ought to be stated is that the house is the seat of Earl Balfour, one of the foremost and most famous men in the world, while a second but important thing is that the middle syllable of the name of the house is pronounced as when a bracing breeze brings a *tinge* of colour to the face.

Whittingehame Tower, the mediæval predecessor of the present house, stands in the grounds, still inhabited, looking strong enough to stand for centuries yet, and full of historical memories, of which one is that the Earl of Bothwell and his friends met there to arrange the death of Darnley. So goes the tradition, if it be nothing more.

There are long avenues approaching the house on either side, through grounds which are remarkably well wooded and diversified by height and hollow and a river glen. The river is known as Whittingehame Water, but it is the same stream which is known earlier as Garvald Water, and on the neighbouring estate of Beil as the Beil Burn. It ultimately falls into Belhaven Bay near Dunbar as the Belton Water.

The house is a very large mansion, built in the classical style. Its main front may be called north, though it actually faces north-east. And it is of impressive length. On this front the principal place in the design goes to the high central block, which has a slightly lower extension on each side. The central block comprises three storeys, the middle part of the lowest storey fronted by a porch which projects well in advance of the building and has a canopy supported by a row of four graceful fluted columns of the Doric order, after the style of the beautiful and well-preserved Temple of Theseus at Athens. That temple was built about 465 B.C., and by reason of its excellent preservation has been a model for much modern classical architecture. The columns of the Whittingehame porch have plain slab capitals and support an entablature of correct character. The columns are all in front, and the need of columns at the sides is obviated by a three-sided structure at the angles slightly lower than the porch. Each of these three sides has a window, and the divisions between the sides are surmounted by the Greek urn or covered vase. This feature is an alteration made less than thirty years ago, previous to which vehicles drove under the porch. Plain windows, string courses between the storeys, and parapets of classical balusters, are the general notes of the whole front. Two mullioned windows above the porch are an exception, and most of the windows have plain mouldings above them.

Generally speaking, this description applies also to the south front. But in a position corresponding to the porch on the north front the south front has a rounded apsidal window with a classical balustraded parapet above it and a series of steps in front of it, leading down to a terrace enclosed by a similar balustrade. About the middle of the terrace is a sundial, and the front of the terrace is several feet above the ground, which extends to the south. This side appears to have a storey more than the north. That is due to the removal of a depth of about 6 feet of soil on the south side, the soil being used to widen the terrace, which is a very attractive feature of that front.

The arrangement of the rooms is very simple and symmetrical. On passing between the columns of the entrance we are in a porch with a marble floor, the walls decorated with guns, shields, and sword bayonets. Going forward, we enter a hall which is approximately square, forming an inner hall and a billiard-room. A reminder of the Great War is here on the wall, now framed and on the right of the fireplace—the flag of a German submarine captured by the British and French off Havre on April 5, 1916. On either side of it is a sword and sheath, and below it, also framed, are three things—in the centre a coat of arms with two lions " rampant regardant," crowned. On each side, in a separate panel, is an eagle with spread wings—" displayed " is perhaps the heraldic term. One of the swords was presented to Lord Balfour's nephew by the inhabitants of Nedjef in Mesopotamia. The other was given to Lord Balfour by the officers in command of the armoured cars in Armenia before the Russian collapse. The coats of arms were taken off enemy motor cars abandoned when the British advanced into Bulgaria.

Behind the square hall is a long corridor or gallery, which runs from end to end of the house, and from which the principal rooms are entered—the dining-room on the right at the front, the library

WHITTINGEHAME
THE SOUTH FRONT

WHITTINGEHAME TOWER

similarly at the back : the drawing-room on the left at the back, and other rooms on the front. The two ground floor windows on the extreme left of the north front and that adjacent to them round the angle in the east end have a special interest in that they are the windows of Lord Balfour's own study. A room on the ground floor of the south front, between the drawing-room and the library, and with the apsidal window looking out on the steps, is the music-room.

The old tower deserves some notice. If we follow the sloping ground to a rustic bridge which crosses the river to the west we shall reach it. The entrance is at the east end and has the Douglas coat of arms above it. The ground floor is vaulted, and the first floor contains the ancient hall, which has a beautiful ceiling of plaster moulding like those at Winton House, evidently done about the same time by the same artists. There can be no doubt that the tower dates at the latest from the fifteenth century.

The Earls of March held baronial courts there. In 1372, George, Earl of March, gave the Manor of Whittingehame to his sister Agnes when she married James Douglas, of Dalkeith ; and the Douglases held the lands for about 190 years from that time. In October, 1564, Queen Mary granted to James, Earl of Morton, as representing the Douglases of Dalkeith, all their estates, including the barony of Whittingehame.

The most famous and gruesome association of the tower with Scottish history is that of the meeting of Bothwell, Morton, and Archibald Douglas, said to have taken place in the first week of December, 1566, in the tower, to arrange for the murder of Darnley.

Early in the seventeenth century Viscount Seton of Kingston married the daughter of Sir Archibald Douglas, and through her as heiress Whittingehame became a Seton property. Their youngest daughter inherited the property and married William Hay, of Drummelzier, second son of the 1st Earl of Tweeddale, in 1695. It continued in that family until 1817, when it was sold to James Balfour, second son of John Balfour of Balbirnie. The present beautiful house was built by him, the architect being Sir Robert Smirke.

An interesting fact is that Traprain Law is on the estate, and that it was with Lord Balfour's permission and encouragement that the elaborate series of excavations were made which proved that the Law had been a fortified town in several periods in prehistoric days. *The Treasure of Traprain*, by O. E. Curle, published in 1923, gives a fascinating account of the work and of the discoveries of wonderful silver vessels, with fine engraving, some of it Byzantine, some of it ecclesiastical, and all of it plunder of rich cities or houses, perhaps monasteries. The plunderers were doubtless Norsemen, who used Traprain as their piratical seat, and for some reason had not been able to carry off their spoil when they made a hurried departure, although they had it ready, the beautiful vessels crushed out of shape to be more easily removed for melting.

XLIX

WINTON HOUSE, PENCAITLAND, EAST LOTHIAN

WINTON HOUSE is situated in a very charming park, of which one of the gates opens on the road a few yards from the very small village of Pencaitland. In the opposite direction it is thirteen miles from Edinburgh. The Winton estate is not now large, but the park is wonderfully beautiful, especially in the autumn, when the dying and falling leaves give it a great variety of colouring. The house is considerably above sea-level on ground which slopes up from the Firth of Forth towards the foot of the Lammermuir Hills, and yet it is only four miles in a straight line from the sea.

On account of its situation it has a certain amount of literary interest as having been identified with the " Ravenswood " of Sir Walter Scott's romance, *The Bride of Lammermuir*. Sir Walter described the position : " In the gorge of a pass or mountain glen, ascending from the fertile plains of East Lothian, there stood in former times an extensive castle, of which only the ruins are now visible." But there is no gorge ; there is no mountain glen ; and it never was " an extensive castle." With a very fair knowledge of all the country round about, I cannot give way to the temptation of saying that the identification is correct.

The house was built in the year 1620, but it looks very different now from what it did when first built, on account of additions of a much later date. These are chiefly on the north side, which contains the entrance. Fortunately they are not as high as the original building; therefore, although they conceal the lower parts of the original walls, the structure of the house as it was first raised is clearly to be seen. In that condition it takes the old Scottish form, of which there remain some unaltered examples, of the capital **L**. The longer block extends from west to east, and the shorter goes north from the east end of the other. If they were sides of a rectangle, the long block would be south and the short block east. There may have been a tower or other small building forming a wing at the west end, and a wall to enclose a courtyard, thus making a north side to the oblong. In the angle formed by the two blocks in the court-yard there would be a round tower or turret, either rising from the foundation or corbelled out at the top of the first storey.

That is a picture of Winton House as it was built by William Wallace in 1620, when he was King's Master Mason and Architect, for George, 10th Lord Seton and 3rd Earl of Winton, and his wife, Anne Hay. Wallace was a burgess of Edinburgh in 1621, and the first builder of Heriot's Hospital. He also did work in Edinburgh Castle and Holyrood Palace. There was some sort of a house on the site in earlier days, and it is just possible that part of the old walls may have been used in the new work. The building of 1620 became partly ruinous towards the end of the eighteenth century, after many years of neglect while it was part of the attainted and confiscated estates of the Earl of Winton. After 1780 it was bought by Hamilton of Pencaitland, and Colonel Hamilton built the additions which made the house what it is at present.

Looking at the north front, where our old conjectural wall would be, we see a long line in the castellated style. The house looks in this view as if it had been built in three tiers, one behind another, and the furthest the building of 1620. The front tier is one storey high, with an octagonal tower at each end a little higher than the rest of the line. The centre of the line is broken by the projection of an entrance tower of two storeys in height, covering the east half of the old courtyard, so that the whole of that courtyard has been taken into the house. The later part of the house is easily distinguished by its castellated character and its crenellated parapets—the Gothic of the date of its additions, as contrasted with the old Scottish domestic style of the early building.

The style of Lord Winton's building is clearly seen now on the east end, where there used to be an elaborate and large conservatory completely killing the beauty of the old work. The present laird, Mr. Gilbert Ogilvy, who is a trained architect with a keen eye for beauty in stone, has removed the conservatory to the great advantage of that east end. A crow-stepped gable is one of the old features, and contains a window of a specially beautiful and characteristic type. In the adjoining part is a window of corresponding design. The special features are the fluted pilasters with capitals, forming the sides of the windows, and the pediments, one of them curved and the other triangular and open at the top. Above the gable rises a stack of five chimneys, tall, made of stone, and carrying a fluted spiral design round them. The end of that east block which faces north also has a crow-stepped gable, with the same number of chimneys of the same type.

The upper part of the original north front has decorative windows similar in design to those described, but with much more elaborate pediments. Two of them have a stack of three chimneys rising

WINTON HOUSE
THE NORTH FRONT

WINTON HOUSE
THE EAST END

from between them, two of them fluted and the other carrying a very detailed leaf design. In one of the pediments is the monogram G.E.W.A.H., with perhaps S in it also, surmounted by an Earl's coronet. On the south side there has been little alteration of the original features of the building. But the ground was a rough steep slope, and it remained so until the house became the property of the late Lady Ruthven. She turned the slope into garden terraces with walks which lead down to the garden and to the meadows which lie by the side of the River Tyne.

The interiors of some of the rooms have been modernised, but the original beauty has been preserved. The ceilings are an outstanding feature, those of the drawing-room and King Charles's room, which is the library, being most elaborate. They are of the same type as some of the beautiful ceilings of Holyrood Palace, and were designed by the same architect. The drawing-room ceiling is especially fine, but King Charles's room has the advantage of great plaster pendants which give it a distinct character of its own. The centre panel of the drawing-room ceiling contains the Seton arms, with many heraldic devices around it, and the monogram of the builder and his wife.

The estates of which Winton was only a part were held by the family of De Quincey in the reign of Alexander I. and later. In that reign one of them was Earl of Winchester in England and at the same time Constable of Scotland. Alexander I. died in 1124, which gives that family an early date. Janet, a daughter of Roger de Quincey the Constable, married Dougal Saytun, the first of the Seton family whose name we know. He is said to have been a member of one of two English-Norman families of the name, and to have been the grandson of one who came to Scotland and received a grant of land which he called " Say-tun," taking his name as De Saytun. It may be so, but Dougal was a strange name for a Norman, and seems to indicate a quickness to intermarry with the Celts, if Dougal was not really a member of a normalised Celtic family.

In the wars of King Robert Bruce, the Quinceys took the losing side, and the Seton of the day took the winning side, chiefly because Bruce was his uncle. So he got the great barony of Tavernent, or Tranent, which was the making of the family. Seton Palace, not far from Winton, was their great place. Nothing now remains of it except a " roundel " at a corner of the garden of the modern Seton Castle. After the attainder the Palace was sold to Alexander Mackenzie, of Portmore, who pulled down the whole magnificent building.

The roundel is historical, for it was there that James VI. halted on meeting the funeral procession of the Earl of Winton, as the King was setting out on his progress to assume the English throne.

Colonel Hamilton of Pencaitland was succeeded by his sister, Mrs. Hamilton Campbell, of Shawfield. She left the place by will to her daughter, Lady Ruthven. She left it to the late Mrs. Nisbet Hamilton Ogilvy, of Belhaven and Dirleton, who in turn left it to the present laird, Gilbert Francis Molyneux Ogilvy, a son of the late Sir Reginald Ogilvy, Baronet, of Inverquharity.

L

YESTER HOUSE, GIFFORD, EAST LOTHIAN

YESTER HOUSE, the residence of the Marquis of Tweeddale, looks an exceedingly modern house. The stonework is so fresh and clean that it might have been built only forty or fifty years ago ; but the truth is that it was begun before 1745, and was finished in that year by William Adam the architect, whose two sons continued his fame. It is said that the workmen who were putting the slates on the roof threw some of them at dragoons fleeing from the battlefield of Prestonpans.

The length of the house is from west to east, and the architectural front faces the north, but the entrance is on the west, by a handsome porch which projects a long distance, carried on square columns, four on each side. From the porch a classical balustrade extends along the ground on either side to the terminations of that west front. The whole of the porch is roofed with glass, and the forward part is open at front and sides. The inner part has its sides filled in with glass, so that it is light, airy, and attractive.

The ground on the north side slopes down from the house, and thus this front receives the advantage of additional height. The centre piece is classical in style, while immediately beneath it the ground is cut away to form a passage which proceeds under the house by a wide classical arch. The ground immediately in front of the south and east parts is beautifully laid out in flower beds and tennis courts, with numerous stone vases on pedestals and with a fountain playing near the tennis courts. It is a very good example of the early Scottish classical style which William Adam inherited from his master, Sir William Bruce, of Kinross.

The general height of the building is two storeys. The slated roof slopes up for some distance and then gives place to a flat roof, while curious attic windows peer out from the slated roof in a row which passes all round the house, thus giving the effect and advantage of another storey. The windows are mostly oblong and square-headed. The middle part of the north face is slightly advanced in front of the general line and has three windows in each storey, with arched heads, while those on the second storey are between square-faced pilasters with Ionic capitals. They rise with the wall at least a complete storey above the general roof line, and support a pediment of which the tympanum contains the arms of the family. There is a middle part of the south front which corresponds with this in style, but is much plainer, with the uppermost part below the plain pediment containing a row of three windows.

It is seldom that one may see a more beautiful or more elegant interior that that of Yester House. From the porch we enter a large and handsome hall. The first part is square ; two columns stand at the further portion of it ; and then it narrows and goes back practically the whole length of the house, ending at a small room, a boudoir, which looks out to the east. At that room it turns or there is an opening on the left from which the grand staircase springs, lighted by a fine dome-shaped elliptical cupola. Several interesting family paintings are here. One of them, by Sir John de Medina, represents the first Marquis and his family, seventeen persons, besides two shown as angels—the reason being obvious. There is an Earl of Dunfermline, by Vandyke, while others are John Napier, of Merchiston and of logarithms, and the Countess of Roxburghe, who was a daughter of the first Marquis and known as " Johnnie Hay's bonnie lass." Many others adorn the staircase.

On the left of the hall as we face the pillars is the library. On the right, entered by doors close to the pillars, are two morning-rooms which communicate with each other. Beyond the morning-room is the billiard-room; and on the left, beyond the library, is the dining-room. The drawing-room is above the library and hall. The arrangement is very regular and symmetrical—a characteristic of houses built on the Scottish classical lines.

A portrait of Lord Charles Hay in one of the morning-rooms recalls a famous incident in which he figured when he commanded the King's company of the Grenadiers at the battle of Fontenoy in 1745. It may best be related in a translation of the words of a French author : " In the midst of that bloody engagement the British and French officers mutually saluted each other by taking off their hats. The English being fifty paces distant from the French and Swiss Guards, Charles Hay, Captain of the English Guards, steps out of the ranks; Count d'Auteroche, Lieutenant of the Grenadiers of the French Guards, goes to meet him. ' Gentlemen of the French Guards,' says the English Captain, 'fire.' 'No, my lord,' answers the Count, ' we never fire first.' The English then gave a running fire. Nineteen officers and 380 soldiers of the French Guard fell dead or wounded, and the Duc de Grammont, colonel of that regiment, was killed." As an example of polite war the incident is perfect.

YESTER HOUSE
FROM THE SOUTH

YESTER HOUSE
THE DRAWING-ROOM FIREPLACE

The drawing-room is the crowning beauty of Yester House and is said to be the finest of its class in Scotland. Its great feature is its mural paintings done in imitation of tapestry. They were done by a French artist, Delacour, in 1761. I believe that they are in the oil medium, flat, rather than in either of the two true forms of fresco, or in *tempera*. It may be noted that almost all modern fresco is done in that way.

A notice of Yester would be incomplete if the story of the " Goblin Hall," to which a short reference was made in the chapter on Colstoun, were not more fully told. It is the old Yester Castle, said to have been built about the year 1267, which is hardly likely to be an incorrect date, as John of Fordun, who died about 1385, mentions it in his *Scotichronicon*—to be more precise, it is probably Fordun's " continuator " who wrote the account, Walter Bower, Abbot of Inchcolm.

Sir Hugo de Gifford, the founder of the old castle, was said to be a wizard, and the hall to have been built by spirits under his control. Fordun's words are : " Hugo Gifford de Yester moritur, cujus castrum vel saltem caveam, et donjionem, arte dæmonica antiquæ relationes ferunt fabrifactum, nam ibidem habetur mirabilis specus subterraneus, opere mirifico constructus, magno terrarum spatio protelatus, qui communiter Bo-Hall appellatus est."

Sir Walter Scott in " Marmion," canto iii., stanza 19, describes the building:

> " A wiser never at the hour
> Of midnight spoke the word of power ;
> The same whom ancient records call
> The founder of the Goblin Hall.
> Of lofty roof and ample size,
> Beneath the castle deep it lies ;
> To hew the living rock profound,
> The floor to pave, the arch to round,
> There never toiled a mortal arm—
> It all was wrought by word and charm."

The old castle is a long way up the Hopes Water from the modern house, and there is not much of it left. But what there is tells of strength, and the " Goblin Hall " is still there, beyond the walls of the castle, beneath the ground, and now entered from the north wall by a doorway to which steps lead down from the courtyard. For centuries the steps were buried, but they were dug out in 1861. The hall is 37 feet long, 13 broad, and 19 in height to the apex of the pointed arch of the vaulted roof. It is unlike anything in Scotland, but it is said to have its parallel at Arques and Roches Guyon in France. Tradition has it that any member of the Hay family interfering with the castle is doomed to a sudden death; and the tradition was fulfilled when the stair to the Bo Hall was opened up in 1861 by the Lord Gifford of that day.

The Hays are descended from William de Haya, Royal Butler to Malcolm IV. and William the Lion, which takes us back to about the year 1160. In the fourteenth century Sir William Hay married the heiress of Sir John Gifford, of Yester, and the estate has remained in the Hay family ever since. The original peerage of Lord Hay of Yester dates from 1487, the Earldom of Tweeddale from 1646, and the Marquisate from 1694. The present Marquis is the 11th, and it is interesting to realise that he is a descendant of that wizard knight or baron who built Bo Hall. King Alexander III. visited him in his den to inquire his fortune before he met the wild King Haco of Norway in battle near Largs. And in the stanza following that already quoted, Scott tells what happened when the King's bugles sounded outside Sir Hugo's castle:

> " Lord Gifford, deep beneath the ground,
>   Heard Alexander's bugle sound
>   And tarried not his garb to change,
>   But in his wizard habit strange
>   Came forth—a quaint and fearful sight."

WORKS CONSULTED BY THE AUTHOR

NISBET : *System of Heraldry.*

SOCIETY OF ANTIQUARIES OF SCOTLAND : *Proceedings.*

HUME OF GODSCROFT : *History of the House of Douglas.*

MRS. WARE SCOTT : *Lamington : Past and Present.*

ANDREW WYNTON : *Orygynale Cronykil of Scotland.*

CALDERWOOD : *History of the Kirk of Scotland.*

A. O. CURLE : *The Treasure of Traprain.*

HEW HAMILTON DALRYMPLE : *Account of Oxenfoord Castle.*

Burke's Peerage.

JOHN DE FORDUN : *Chronica Gentis Scotorum (The Scotichronicon).*

PATERSON : *History of Ayrshire Families.*

CHALMERS : *Caledonia.*

New Statistical Account of Scotland.

SIR ROBERT SIBBALD : *History of Fife.*

BALFOUR PAUL : *The Scots Peerage.*

BISHOP BURNET : *History of His Own Time.*

JAMES GRANT : *Old and New Edinburgh.*

KAY : *Edinburgh Portraits.*

PINKERTON : *Select Scottish Ballads.*

DEAN RAMSAY : *Reminiscences of Scottish Life and Character.*

SIR WALTER SCOTT : *Marmion ; Bride of Lammermuir ; Tales of a Grand-father ; Castle Dangerous ; Border Minstrelsy.*

BYRON : *English Bards and Scotch Reviewers.*

JOHN RUSSELL : *The Haigs of Bemersyde.*

INDEX

INDEX

INDEX